7

COPY 1

641.5
M   MERAS, PHYLLIS
       CARRY-OUT CUISINE
     1695

Carry-Out Cuisine

Also by Phyllis Méras

First Spring: A Martha's Vineyard Journal

A Yankee Way with Wood

Miniatures: How to Make Them, Use Them, Sell Them

Vacation Crafts

Christmas Angels (with Juliana Turkevich)

The Mermaids of Chenonceaux and 828 Other Tales: An Anecdotal Guide to Europe

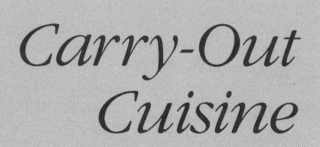

Carry-Out Cuisine

Phyllis Méras

with Frances Tenenbaum

Houghton Mifflin Company   Boston
1982

For Ruth Roberts,
an enviable cook

Library of Congress Cataloging in Publication Data

Méras, Phyllis.
    Carry-out cuisine.

    Includes index.
    1. Cookery.   2. Grocery trade—United States.   I. Tenen-
baum, Frances.   II. Title.
TX652.M45   1982   641.5   82-9327
ISBN 0-395-32212-X   AACR2
ISBN 0-395-33010-6 pbk.

Printed in the United States of America

V 10 9 8 7 6 5 4 3 2 1

Acknowledgments

For their assistance in gathering the material for this book, I am grateful to Anne Allen, Jana Allen, Stephanie Bruno, Eileen Chambers, Marylin Chou, Beatrice Freeman, Barbara Hess, Bill Hibbard, Holly Higinbotham, Elizabeth Ann Johnson, Bruce Kohlen, Carolyn Levin, Beatrice MacDonald, Georgia O'Connor, Erma Perry, Virginia Poole, Susan St. Angelo, Vicki Saunders, Janet Steinberg, Gerry Reedy, Patricia Rich, Jean Rossi, Judy Thorne, Robert Tolf, and Richard Walton.

And I am especially grateful to my editor, Linda Glick; not only was this book her idea, but, as a talented cook, she tested many of the recipes.

Phyllis Méras

Contents

Foreword

Wherever they live, followers of what's new in food fashions are familiar with names like Dean & DeLuca of New York, San Francisco's Oakville Grocery, Jamail's in Houston. These gourmet food shops and scores like them all over the country represent an important trend in convenience food preparation — a far cry from the proverbial pizza, fried chicken, or "Chinese" to go. For those of you who are able to frequent take-out food shops, this book makes favorite recipes available for the first time. For those who may not live near enough to patronize these delectable emporia, it allows you to create carry-out cuisine in your own kitchen. The recipes included are the most sought-after choices of people all over the country who care about eating well — they have stood the test of popular demand.

These recipes are perfect for informal entertaining — for brunches, buffets, small dinner parties, cocktail parties. Since take-out shops prepare everything in advance, all the recipes are for dishes that the working host or hostess can make ahead. Many can be frozen. All the dishes are interesting and special, but they vary in the degree of time and expertise needed to prepare them. The cook with experience might like to try an elegant seafood mousse or a hunter's pâté. For the less experienced, there are equally delicious but considerably less difficult first courses — eggplant caviar, for example, or smoked bluefish spread.

The recipes have been tested, and edited for style and consistency; but I have not attempted to make basic procedures uniform throughout. This means that there are several different versions of pie crust, for instance, all of which seem to work well. The current popularity of certain foods — pasta salads, poultry, seafood, and chocolate — is evident throughout the book. Chicken salad, a perennial favorite, is offered in three up-to-the-minute variations, and there are six deliciously different recipes for chocolate cake.

In researching this work, visiting kitchens on the West Coast and the East and in between, I have been struck by the wide range of people who are the owners of gourmet take-out food shops. There are the expected French chefs, of course, but there are also former ballet dancers and medievalists, business executives and housewives, schoolteachers and advertising men. Most are young and adventuresome, filled with enthusiasm for good food and good company. Their shops and their creations reflect that enthusiasm. Invariably, the shops are invitingly stylish and the ingredients required in the dishes fresh and healthful (though the cholesterol-conscious should be wary of the occasional abundance of butter and cream).

In choosing shops — and recipes — I have borne in mind the national interest in regional as well as gourmet cooking, so from San Francisco comes a recipe for a persimmon salad (in nonpersimmon country, pears may be substituted). New England's gourmet take-out shops contribute lobster bisque and scallop chowder and oyster stew. A Florida kitchen offers a Key lime pie. There is an international flavor to much gourmet cooking, too, so there are recipes here for delicate French pastries, hearty Hungarian stews, and German potato salads.

In preparing this book, I have eaten well, and so, I hope, will all those who use it. *Bon appétit!*

Phyllis Méras

A Regional Listing of Shops and Recipes

NEW YORK

New York City

Abbondanza
Spinach and Egg Drop Soup

Balducci's
Chicken Tarragon
Pasticcio

Dean & DeLuca
Chicken Escabeche
Stuffed Flank Steak
Duck in Campari
Strawberry Tart

Délices la Côte Basque
Visidantine
Eugénie

Demarchelier
Bay Scallops with Endive
Choucroute Garnie
Spiral Pasta Salad

E.A.T.
Shrimp Frittata
Smoked Whitefish Salad
Cheddar Cheese Muffins
Cheese Cake

Neuman & Bogdonoff
Oyster Stew I
Swordfish Croquettes
Chicken, Shrimp, and Scallop
    Provençal
Celeriac Rémoulade

The Silver Palate
Braised Leeks with Champagne
    Butter Sauce
Pear and Endive Salad
Incredible Chocolate Mousse
    Cake

Les Trois Petit Cochons Charcuterie
Scallop Mousse

Washington Market
Breast of Chicken with
    Prosciutto and Sage
Seafood Pasta Salad
Broccoli with Lemon and
    Olive Oil
Poached Pears on a Bed of
    Apple Purée

Zabar's
Antipasto Salad
Lox and Onion Quiche
German-Style Potato Salad

Long Island

A la Carte at Gilliewrinkles
Spinach Phyllo
Baked Veal Marden
Galettes au Fromage

Caviar Etcetera
Sautéed Breast of Chicken
   Smitane
Caviar-Style Duckling
Pesto

Les Chefettes
Eggplant Caviar
Breast of Chicken Marsala
Curried Crab Meat
Apricot Mousse

Gourmet Pasta
Lime Veal with Kiwi
Tomato-Olive Pasta Sauce
   (Sauce Savoia)

Jonathan's
Curried Chicken Salad

Prime Concern
Santorini Salad
Artichoke and Carrot Salad

NEW ENGLAND

Boston—Cambridge

The Black Forest
Lobster Salad
Pesto Tortellini

Pasta Salad with Spinach and
   Feta Cheese
Oriental Chicken
Sugar Snap Peas and
   Raspberries

The Fishmonger
Smoked Bluefish Spread
Oyster Stew II
Shellfish Gazpacho
Scallop and Shrimp Casserole
Bluefish and Mussels with
   Mustard Sauce
Squid Salad with Vegetables
Mussel and Pasta Salad

Formaggio Kitchen
Chicken Liver Mousse
Chicken Indienne
Cheese Tortellini
Broccoli-Mushroom Salad
Lemon Poppy-Seed Teacake
Orange Chocolate Teacake

Rebecca's
Marinated Chicken Wings
Curried Shrimp and Rice Salad
Orzo Salad
Brussels Sprouts Salad
Ginger Pear Pie

Lexington

Goodies to Go
Lemon Sesame Chicken
Tomato and Dill Quiche
Cream of Carrot with Dill Soup

Saucy Stuffed Chicken
Chicken and Broccoli Salad
Eggplant Provençal
Shrimp and Feta Pasta Sauce
Granny's Goodies
Lemony Raisin Pie
Berries' Favorite Shortcake

Wellesley

The Charcuterie
French Onion Tart
Swedish Potted Beef with
    Lingonberries and
    Horseradish
Scottish Shortbread

Martha's Vineyard

Poole's Fish Market
Quahaug Chowder
Fisherman's Stew
Mussel Chowder

Providence, Rhode Island

The Providence Cheese—Tavola Calda
Providence Cheese Quiche

MID-ATLANTIC

Washington, D.C.

The American Café Market
Cream of Broccoli Soup
Seafood Gumbo
Seafood Salad
Sesame Noodle Salad

Chicken Tarragon II
Potato Salad without
    Mayonnaise

Fête Accomplie
Cold Curried Fish
Easy Beef Stew
Moroccan Kefta

Pasta, Inc.
Winter Tomato Sauce
Mushroom Sauce à la Veronese
Shrimp Sauce

Sutton Place Gourmet
Crab Roulade
Smoked Salmon Mousse

Suzanne's
Torta Rustica
Curried Chicken Salad I

The Watergate Chefs
Salmon Steaks with Golden
    Caviar and Parsley Sauce
Vegetable Salad in Creamy
    Vinaigrette

Philadelphia

Cynthia Cariseo Café
Poached Pears in Chocolate
    Sauce

The Fruit Lady
Hunter's Pâté
Split Pea Soup Jardinière
Milanese Pesto Soup
Creole Fish Stew
Mediterranean Pasta Salad

Piper's Potpourri
Walnut Sauce

The Market of the
Commissary
Chicken Satay with Peanut
 Sauce
Lamb Curry with Eggplant
Sweet-Sour Cucumber Salad

A Moveable Feast
Lobster Bisque
Chicken Kuwayaki
Apple Cake

The Public Cookshop
Flautas
Potage Provençal
Curried Chicken Salad II

SOUTH AND SOUTHWEST

Atlanta

Proof of the Pudding
Corn Chowder
Quick Chicken Curry

Boca Raton, Florida

Campbell and Co.'s
"A Matter of Taste"
Chicken and Sausage Gumbo
Mexican Braided Bread with
 Brie
Fudge Squares

Miami, Florida

McMead's
Picadillo
Rice Salad with Peanuts and
 Snow Peas
Honey-Glazed Carrot Salad
Rugelach
Carrot Cake

Naples, Florida

The Chef's Garden and
Truffles
Smoked Trout Mousse
Chocolate Grand Marnier Cake
Chocolate Cheese Cake

Sanibel, Florida

Si Bon
Sautéed Shrimp with Zucchini
Spicy Mustard
Frozen Key Lime Pie

Tampa, Florida

The Deli at Ybor Square
Strawberries Olé

Houston

Jim Jamail & Sons Food
Market
Mexican Shrimp Salad
Black-Eyed Pea and Ham Salad
Mexican Pineapple-Cabbage
 Salad

Ouisie's Table and the Traveling Brown Bag Lunch Co.
Shrimp Ouisie
Mushroom Vinaigrette

New Orleans

La Marquise
Couronne des Rois
Gâteau Pithiviers

Scottsdale, Arizona

marché Gourmet
Straw and Hay Salad
Duck and Pheasant Salad

MIDWEST

Ann Arbor

Complete Cuisine Ltd.
Poulet Dijonnaise
Spanakopita

Chicago

Kenessey Gourmets Internationale
Hungarian Beef Goulash
Pork Roast Stuffed with Smoked
  Sausage

Lisi's Hors d'Oeuvre Bakery
Pâte à Choux with Chicken
  Chutney Filling
Shrimp Quiche Creole

Mitchell Cobey Cuisine
Tabbouleh
Apple Tart

Cincinnati

Alesci's International Foods
Marinated Octopus Salad
Caponata
Stuffed Grape Leaves
Baklava

Glencoe, Illinois

La Belle Cuisine
Mousse de Poisson
Cream of Asparagus and Morel
  Soup
Lemon Tart

Prairie Village, Kansas

The Gourmet Grocer
Gingered Pear Salad

Kansas City, Missouri

Pasta Presto
Praline Cheesecake

Minneapolis

Le Petit Chef
Cucumber Bisque
Rabbit with Apricots
Light Chocolate Cake
Quick Chocolate Mousse

WEST COAST

Los Angeles

Bagatelle
Fish Pâté
Cold Asparagus Soup
Chestnut and Chocolate Cake

Mangia
Semolina Gnocchi
Stuffed Boned Leg of Lamb
Roasted Red and Green Bell
  Peppers
Raspberry Tart

Le Marmiton
Artichokes Greek-Style

San Francisco

Fettuccine Bros.
Italian Chicken Salad
Marinara Sauce

Maggie Gin's Pure and Fresh Chinese Country Cooking Restaurant
Chinese Chicken Salad

The Oakville Grocery Company
Black Beans with Andouille
  Sausage
Wild Rice with Shiitake
  Mushrooms
Persimmon Salad

Vivande
Capunatina (Sicilian Eggplant
  Relish)

Pollo al Limone (Lemon
  Chicken)
White Bean Caviar Salad
Amaretti (Almond Cookies)
Pere Ripieni (Stuffed Pears)

Berkeley

Poulet
Stuffed Chicken Breasts with
  Lemon Caper Sauce
Zucchini Mufaletta Salad

San Diego

Piret's
Rarebit Quiche
Artichoke Heart and Feta
  Cheese Quiche
Herb and Three-Cheese Quiche

Seattle

Gretchen's Of Course
Green Peppercorn Terrine
Pasta Primavera
Ziti Salad with Sausage
Ratatouille
Hot Fudge Pudding Cake

Rex's Market Delicatessen
Chicken Liver Pâté
Cold Raspberry Soup
Pork and Apricot Stew

Tacoma

The Chaplain's Pantry
Lentil Soup
Beef in Burgundy
Lamb and Artichoke Stew

xvi

Appetizers and First Courses

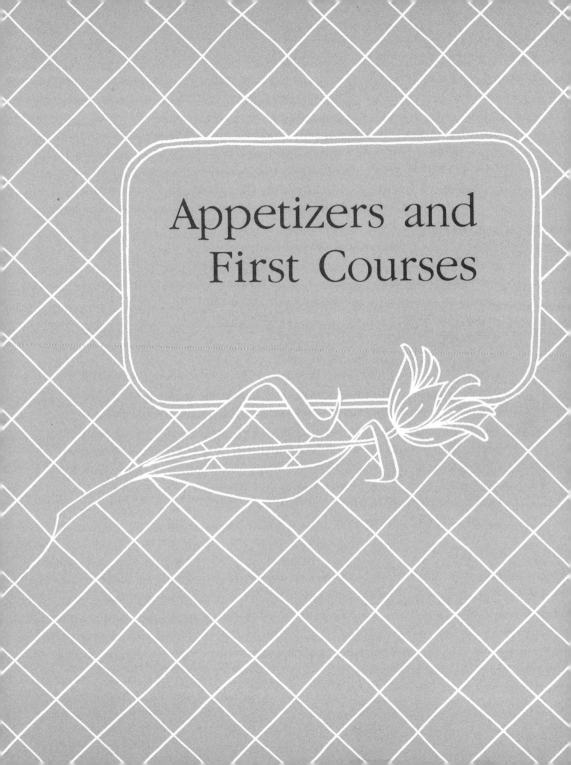

Marinated Octopus Salad

Serves 8 to 10

ALESCI'S INTERNATIONAL FOODS, CINCINNATI

Every year at holiday time, Alesci's has fresh *anguilla* (eel), *seppia* (cuttlefish), *raia* (skate), *calamari* (squid), and *polpi* (octopus, which is the main ingredient of this salad). For the vigil of Christmas on Christmas Eve, when an all-fish menu is traditional in many Italian families, this octopus salad is often the appetizer.

4 small octopi
5 fresh lemons
3 ounces mixed pickling spice
2 cups olive oil
1 cup lemon juice

1 tablespoon salt (or to taste)
1 teaspoon freshly ground
    black pepper (or to taste)
Parsley sprigs (for garnish)

Cover the octopi with cold water into which you have squeezed 4 whole lemons. When the lemons are squeezed, quarter the remains and add them to the water along with the pickling spice. Bring the water to a boil; then turn the heat to low and simmer for at least 1 hour. The octopi are done when a tentacle, cut off and put under cold water to cool, peels easily. When this happens, remove the octopi from the water, cool, peel, and cut into small pieces. Combine with the olive oil, lemon juice, salt, and pepper. Garnish with parsley sprigs and the fifth lemon, sliced. Serve chilled.

Antipasto Salad

ZABAR'S, NEW YORK CITY (UPPER WEST SIDE)

In 1936, Louis Zabar opened his first appetizer-grocery store on the Upper West Side of Manhattan. In 1950, when he died, his sons sold all but the present store at Eightieth Street and Broadway. Today, that extensive store sells more than forty kinds of bread and twenty different goat cheeses, hundreds of sausages, and thousands of articles for preparing and processing foods. Among the gourmet take-out items sold at Zabar's is this antipasto salad.

½ small head cauliflower
½ cup artichoke hearts
1 large onion, sliced
½ cup baby corn
½ cup hot green chili peppers
½ cup sliced carrots
½ cup chopped celery
½ cup chopped green olives

½ cup ripe black olives
2 teaspoons drained capers
¼ cup red wine vinegar
¾ cup olive oil
1 clove garlic, crushed
¼ teaspoon freshly ground black pepper

Break the cauliflower into small pieces. In a large bowl, combine the flowerets with the other vegetables, the olives, and the capers. Be sure everything has been well drained. Shake the vinegar, olive oil, garlic, and pepper in a jar, and pour it over the vegetables. Let the salad marinate in the refrigerator for 48 hours before serving.

Flautas

THE PUBLIC COOKSHOP, PHILADELPHIA

The Public Cookshop, on Pine Street in the heart of Philadelphia, specializes in preparing good food for busy young professionals with a taste for gourmet cuisine but no time to prepare it. Eighty percent of its patrons are steady customers, a clear indication that its dedicated, hard-working owners, Deborah Baldwin and Kirk Rynearson, are doing something right. *Flautas* are a transplant from Mexico, and are just as good for lunch as they are before dinner.

30 wheat flour (not corn) tortillas, for wrapping

Grated cheese (about 1 pound)

Picadilla Filling

4 pounds hot Italian sausages

3 pounds mixed ground veal, pork, and beef

1 pound onions, chopped

4 cups ketchup

¼ cup brown sugar

2 cups chopped green olives

1 cup sliced blanched almonds

2 tablespoons chili powder

1 tablespoon ground cinnamon

1 tablespoon minced garlic

2 cups raisins, macerated in sherry to cover while you are sautéing the meats and onion

Sauté the sausages. When they are cooked, remove the casing and chop the meat. Meanwhile, sauté the ground meat and onions. Drain them. Combine all these ingredients with all the remaining filling ingredients. Put ¼ cup of filling in the center of each tortilla, folding in the edges of the tortilla to make a square package. Place the packages on a greased baking sheet, seam side down. Top them with grated cheese and bake in a preheated 400° oven for 15 minutes. *Flautas* are excellent served with a dollop of sour cream.

Smoked Bluefish Spread
Serves 10 to 12

THE FISHMONGER, CAMBRIDGE

Here's a new hors d'oeuvre popular in seacoast resorts where the fishermen are bringing in more bluefish than can be consumed fresh. You can mix this spread by hand, or in a food processor.

½ pound smoked bluefish (or a little more)

1 pound cream cheese, softened

2 tablespoons minced red pepper

2 tablespoons minced red onion

2 tablespoons finely chopped parsley

1 heaping teaspoon Pommery mustard

½ teaspoon horseradish

2 tablespoons sour cream

Salt and freshly ground black pepper to taste

Take the skin off the bluefish. Break the fish into pieces in a good-sized bowl. Add the other ingredients and mix well. Taste for seasonings and adjust if necessary. Refrigerate until cold. Serve with crackers.

The Silver Palate

Capunatina (Sicilian Eggplant Relish)

VIVANDE, SAN FRANCISCO   *Serves 6 generously*

Carlo Middione, the bearded chef-proprietor of San Francisco's Vivande, is a strong proponent of Sicilian cooking, which, he frequently points out to his patrons, need not be heavy with olive oil and garlic and tomato paste, but can be subtle indeed. His eggplant relish, which is a great appetizer but also makes a fine light supper or lunch, proves his point.

1 large eggplant, diced into medium-sized pieces with the skin on

⅓ cup olive oil for frying (more if needed)

1 large Spanish onion, coarsely chopped

3 medium fresh tomatoes, skinned and coarsely chopped; or 1 15-ounce can whole tomatoes, coarsely chopped

1 or 2 tablespoons tomato paste (optional)

1 scant tablespoon wine vinegar

⅓ cup pitted black olives, sliced

⅓ cup pitted green olives, sliced

1½ tablespoons capers

Salt and freshly ground black pepper to taste

2 tablespoons pine nuts, slightly toasted

½ cup diced celery, lightly sautéed

White or black raisins soaked in several changes of water for 20 minutes to remove some of the sugar

Crayfish tails or lobster tails or tuna packed in oil are optional additions for a Palermo-style *capunatina*

Brown the diced eggplant in the olive oil over a very fast flame. Do not overcook it. Set it aside. Sauté the onions over a moderate flame until they are transparent but not brown. Set them aside. Combine the eggplant and onions with the rest of the ingredients (except the

6

optional seafood) in a heavy saucepan and cook for 30 minutes or so over a low flame. If adding the seafood, do it only during the last few minutes of cooking, for it cooks rapidly and will continue to cook as the *capunatina* cools off.

In preparing this dish, bear in mind that it should not be over-cooked. Even though well blended, all the ingredients should remain identifiable.

Capunatina may be served hot or cold. As a main course, precede it with a plate of pasta and clams or pasta and pesto or a risotto with chicken broth and cheese. Fresh fruit or a light pastry makes a pleasing finish. When served as a hot vegetable, *capunatina* is an excellent complement to hearty entrées such as lamb chops, meat loaf, and roast chicken. Cold, it is good with tongue, ham, or cold roasts.

Caponata   *Serves 12 to 15*

ALESCI'S INTERNATIONAL FOODS, CINCINNATI

Pat Ciuccio's specialty food and take-out shop is really a family affair. His father, Vito, runs the bakery, where all the breads and pastries sold in the store are baked. His mother supervises the kitchen staff and makes the sauces. Daughter Karen is in charge of catering, and daughter Debbie works in the office (which is managed by Pat's wife, Lillian). Ciuccio's Restaurant, next door to the store, is run by son Jim.

Caponata is one of the specialties listed on the take-out department's chalkboard.

1 stalk celery, coarsely chopped

3 green peppers, chopped

Sufficient olive oil to prevent sticking

3 medium eggplants cut into ¾-inch cubes, unpeeled

2 medium onions, chopped

1 pound mushrooms, chopped

½ cup wine vinegar

1 teaspoon crushed red pepper

2 tablespoons sugar

Salt to taste

1 28-ounce can tomatoes, drained and chopped

½ cup green olives, chopped

½ cup black olives, chopped

Sauté the celery and green peppers in olive oil. Add the eggplant, onions, and mushrooms, and sauté lightly. Add the vinegar, red pepper, sugar, salt, and tomatoes, and cook until the eggplant is tender. Add the olives. Let the mixture stand for half an hour and serve warm — or chill and serve cold.

Spinach Phyllo
Makes 30 to 36 pastries

A LA CARTE AT GILLIEWRINKLES,
  COLD SPRING HARBOR, LONG ISLAND

Although making these phyllo pastries is time-consuming and painstaking work, they freeze beautifully. Place them on cookie sheets until frozen, and then store in foil containers with wax paper between each layer.

6 tablespoons butter

1 generous bunch scallions, finely chopped (leave on 2 inches of the green part)

1 bunch Italian parsley, stems removed, finely chopped

1 medium onion, minced

1 tablespoon dried dill

1 pound fresh spinach, washed and chopped; or 1 package frozen chopped spinach, thawed and drained

1/8 teaspoon salt

1/8 teaspoon cayenne

1/4 teaspoon nutmeg

3 eggs, lightly beaten

3/4 pound feta cheese, coarsely crumbled

1/4 cup bread crumbs

1 1-pound package frozen phyllo pastry sheets, thawed

1 1/4 cups melted butter

Preheat the oven to 425°. Melt the 6 tablespoons butter in a large sauté pan and sauté the scallions, parsley, and onion until all are limp and the onions are golden. Add the dill and spinach and stir until the spinach is wilted. Whisk the salt, cayenne, and nutmeg into the eggs and stir them into the spinach mixture. Add the feta and the bread crumbs. If the mixture seems too moist, add more bread crumbs.

Cover the work surface with heavy-duty foil and secure with tape. Open up the phyllo pastry sheets. Brush the foil with melted butter and spread out one sheet of pastry on it. Brush this with melted butter. Cover the remaining pastry sheets with plastic wrap and a damp towel so they will not dry out.

Cut the pastry sheet into five even strips, lengthwise. At the bottom of one strip place a heaping teaspoon of spinach filling. Fold the pastry over into a triangle. Repeat until the pastry sheets and filling are used up. Place the pastries on a greased baking sheet with sides, and brush the tops with melted butter. Bake immediately for 15 to 20 minutes, or freeze for later use. (The frozen pastries should be defrosted and then baked in a 425° oven for 15 minutes, or until puffed and golden brown.)

Artichokes Greek-Style

Serves 4

LE MARMITON, SANTA MONICA

René Robin left Paris soon after World War II to become a chef at the Ritz Carlton in Montreal. From there, he moved to Romanoff's in Los Angeles; he was later the chef for Dean Martin's Dino's Lodge and for the Jerry Lewis Restaurant. Finally, he started his own restaurant — Le Petit Moulin — in Santa Monica. But six years ago he gave up the restaurant business in favor of a gourmet take-out shop. Today, at Le Marmiton, he produces "the finest of continental cuisine for your home."

2 cups white wine
2 cups water
1 cup lemon juice
1 tablespoon coriander seed
½ teaspoon whole
  peppercorns

3 pinches salt
⅓ teaspoon thyme
2 bay leaves
4 artichokes

Boil together all the ingredients but the artichokes. Meanwhile, cut each artichoke into four or six pieces; cut off the thorns and remove the thistle. Then drop the pieces into the boiling marinade and let them cook for 40 to 50 minutes. When the pieces are very tender, remove and drain them. Chill them in the refrigerator and serve them cold the next day.

Le Marmiton

10

Pâte à Choux with Chicken Chutney Filling

Makes about 100 small puffs

LISI'S HORS D'OEUVRE BAKERY, CHICAGO

It's the chutney that makes the difference in these crisp hors d'oeuvre puffs, according to their creator, Karen Lisi Smith. She and her husband, Bob, have transformed an old A&P into a popular specialty food shop.

Pastry Puffs

1 cup cold water
Dash of salt
Dash of freshly ground black pepper

Pinch of nutmeg
6 tablespoons butter
1 cup all-purpose flour
4 eggs

Heat the water, salt, pepper, nutmeg, and butter to the boiling point. Remove from the heat. Add the flour all at once, stirring with a wooden spoon until the mixture forms a ball. Return the pan to low heat just until the mixture is warm. Add the eggs, one at a time, beating each thoroughly into the mixture. Using a pastry tube with a fluted tip, make 1-inch puffs on an oiled baking sheet. Bake them for 25 minutes in a preheated 375° oven until they are puffed and brown. Turn off the oven and remove the pastries just long enough to make a small slit from top to bottom in the side of each. Return them to the turned off but warm oven, and with the oven door ajar, dry out the pastries for about 10 minutes — until they are hollow and dry on the inside. If you do not wish to fill the puffs immediately, they can be frozen, thawed, and recrisped in a 350° oven for 5 minutes.

11

Filling

4 cups poached, skinned, and chopped chicken breasts

2 teaspoons garlic juice

2 teaspoons salt

1 teaspoon freshly ground black pepper

3 tablespoons curry powder

3 tablespoons lemon juice

1 cup chopped onion

½ cup Major Grey's chutney

½ to 1 teaspoon turmeric (for color)

Enough bottled salad dressing to bind (use Miracle Whip or a similar dressing that is slightly sweeter than mayonnaise)

Mix all the filling ingredients together and fill the puffs.

Lemon Sesame Chicken

Makes approximately 6 dozen appetizers

GOODIES TO GO,
LEXINGTON, MASSACHUSETTS

This sweet-sour appetizer with a Middle Eastern touch reheats nicely the next day.

¾ cup sesame seeds

3 whole chicken breasts, boned

Juice of 6 lemons

6 cloves garlic, minced or crushed

¾ cup tahini paste

1 cup sesame oil

¼ cup soy sauce

½ cup brown sugar

Place the sesame seeds in a preheated 350° oven for 10 to 12 minutes, until brown.

Cut the chicken into 1-inch serving pieces.

Put the lemon juice, garlic, tahini, sesame oil, and soy sauce in a bowl and whisk the mixture until smooth. Place the chicken pieces in this marinade and refrigerate overnight.

When you are ready to serve the chicken, sauté it over medium-high heat with a little of the marinade and the brown sugar until it is brown. Remove the chicken pieces and roll them in the sesame seeds. Spear the chicken pieces with toothpicks and serve them on a platter. If you like, they may be served with a dipping sauce made by whisking together the following ingredients:

⅓ cup sesame oil
Juice of 1 or 2 lemons
2 or 3 cloves garlic, minced
⅓ cup tahini

3 teaspoons soy sauce
Salt and freshly ground black pepper to taste

Marinated Chicken Wings   *Serves 12*
REBECCA'S, BOSTON

Lightly Oriental are these crisp, sweet-sharp chicken wings. They make a fine cocktail party hors d'oeuvre, since they can be prepared the night before or early on the party day and popped into the oven to brown as the guests begin to arrive.

24 chicken wings, broken into
   three pieces each, tips
   discarded
¼ cup *sake*
2 tablespoons soy sauce

2 tablespoons honey
¾ cup orange juice
1 tablespoon minced ginger
3 cloves garlic, minced
¼ cup oil

Marinate the chicken wings in a mixture of all the other ingredients for at least 3 hours, or overnight, in the refrigerator. Remove them from the marinade and bake them on a rack over a pan in a 400° oven until they are nicely browned.

13

Chicken Satay with Peanut Sauce

THE MARKET OF THE COMMISSARY, PHILADELPHIA

A lively newsletter, a yearly calendar with recipes, cooking classes, wine and food festivals — and just about everything else you can think of associated with the pleasures of eating — make the Commissary and its take-out Market one of Philadelphia's most attractive centers for food. This is one of the recipes featured on The Market's newest calendar.

1¼ pounds boneless chicken
   breasts, cut into ½-inch strips

Marinade

2 tablespoons sesame oil
2 tablespoons corn oil
¼ cup sherry
¼ cup soy sauce
1½ teaspoons minced garlic

1½ teaspoons minced ginger
¼ teaspoon salt
¼ teaspoon freshly ground
   black pepper
Dash of Tabasco

Sauce

4 teaspoons corn oil
2 teaspoons sesame oil
½ cup minced red onion
2 tablespoons minced garlic
1 teaspoon minced ginger
1 tablespoon red wine vinegar
1 tablespoon sugar
⅓ cup peanut butter

½ teaspoon ground coriander
3 tablespoons ketchup
⅓ cup hot water
3 tablespoons soy sauce
½ teaspoon freshly ground
   black pepper
1 tablespoon lime juice (optional)
Tabasco to taste

Put the chicken strips in a bowl. Combine all the marinade ingredients and pour the marinade over the chicken. Let it stand for 1 to 12 hours.

To make the sauce, heat the corn oil and sesame oil. Add the onion, garlic, and ginger and sauté for 5 to 7 minutes over medium heat. Add the vinegar and sugar and cook, stirring, for 3 or 4 minutes, until the sauce carmelizes. Off the heat, stir in the remaining ingredients.

Thread the chicken strips onto toothpicks or small wooden skewers. Bake in a preheated 375° oven for about 10 minutes.

Serve the chicken hot, with the peanut sauce as a dip.

Note: You may substitute beef, lamb, shrimp, or scallops for the chicken. Bake beef or lamb for 10 minutes, shrimp or scallops for 5 to 10 minutes.

Eggplant Caviar
Serves 6 to 8

LES CHEFETTES, GREAT NECK, LONG ISLAND

For those who can't afford genuine caviar, Les Chefettes' chefs recommend this tasty, economical substitute. The food processor is ideal for making it.

1 eggplant
Olive oil for coating eggplant
1 onion, finely minced
1 or 2 cloves garlic, crushed
1 tomato, peeled, chopped, and
  drained

1 tablespoon sugar
2 tablespoons vinegar
3 tablespoons olive oil
Salt and freshly ground black
  pepper to taste

Cut the eggplant in half lengthwise. Coat it all over with oil. Place it, skin side down, on an oiled cookie sheet in a preheated 400° oven for 20 minutes. Cool the eggplant, scoop out the flesh, and chop it finely, using a food processor. Add the other ingredients. Mix well, taste for seasonings, and chill. Serve with crackers or pumpernickel bread rounds. Or serve it in an uncooked scooped-out eggplant half.

Shrimp Quiche Creole

Makes about 60 tartlets

LISI'S HORS D'OEUVRE BAKERY, CHICAGO

These spicy little quiches can be made several days before a party and frozen for later use.

Pâte Brisée

3⅓ cups all-purpose flour
1 cup butter
½ cup cold water

2 tablespoons vegetable oil
2 egg yolks

Cut the butter into the flour until the mixture resembles coarse meal. Make a well in the center. In a separate bowl, beat together the cold water, oil, and egg yolks. Slowly pour into the well and mix until the dough holds together. Turn out onto a floured surface. Form the dough into a ball and refrigerate it in plastic wrap until you are ready to use it. Then roll it out on a floured surface and cut the dough into rounds to fit small muffin tins. Grease the tins and fill them with the rolled dough.

Filling

2 cups grated Swiss cheese
1 cup cooked and chopped
 shrimp

1 green pepper, chopped
6 scallions, chopped (including
 the green parts)

Fill the tartlets with the grated cheese. Combine all the other ingredients and add them to the tartlets. The tartlets are now ready for topping.

Topping

3 tablespoons gumbo filé
1 teaspoon cumin
2 teaspoons hot sauce
2 teaspoons garlic juice
4 tablespoons tomato paste
2 teaspoons salt

1 teaspoon freshly ground
  black pepper
¼ teaspoon nutmeg
6 "large" eggs
2 cups half-and-half

Preheat the oven to 400°. Whisk all the ingredients together and pour the mixture into the tartlet shells over the filling. Bake the tartlets at 400° for 10 minutes; then reduce the heat to 350° for 30 minutes. Cool, and remove from the muffin tins. These quiche tarts may easily be frozen for later use.

Semolina Gnocchi   *Serves 6 as a first course*

MANGIA, WEST LOS ANGELES

A plate of gnocchi is often the start of a first-class dinner in northern Italy and the same is possible in this country, thanks to Kathleen Ellsworth's Mangia.

1 quart milk
1 cup fine semolina
3 tablespoons butter
¾ cup grated Parmesan cheese

¼ cup chopped fresh basil
½ cup grated Parmesan cheese
6 tablespoons butter

Heat the milk just to the boiling point. Then lower the heat. Slowly add the semolina to the milk in a fine stream, stirring steadily. The milk will thicken quickly, so be sure to stir constantly to avoid lumps. Add the 3 tablespoons of butter, the basil, and the ¾ cup Parmesan. Stir well. Pour the mixture onto a damp cookie sheet.

17

Flatten it smooth (it should be ⅜ inch thick) and refrigerate it.

When the "dough" is thoroughly chilled and firm, cut rounds 1 to 2 inches in diameter with a cookie cutter dipped in oil. Place the rounds in a buttered baking dish. Top them with the ½ cup grated Parmesan cheese and the 6 tablespoons butter and bake in a pre-heated 400° oven until bubbly and brown. Sprinkle the gnocchi with more chopped basil before serving.

Stuffed Grape Leaves   Stuffs 50 leaves
ALESCI'S INTERNATIONAL FOODS, CINCINNATI

Pat Ciuccio has been in the food business in Cincinnati for thirty-seven years, the last seven as the owner of this ethnic food shop. Although Italian foods lead the list, Alesci's is also the place to find Oriental, German, Mexican, Indian, Jewish, English, and Greek delicacies, such as these stuffed grape leaves.

½ pound uncooked rice, washed
1 medium onion, chopped
½ cup parsley, chopped
5⅓ ounces Romano cheese, grated

2 teaspoons salt, or to taste
1 teaspoon freshly ground black pepper, or to taste
1 pint jar grape leaves
½ cup olive oil, preferably Greek

Mix together the rice, onion, parsley, cheese, and seasonings. Set aside. Lay out the grape leaves and place some of the stuffing on each one. Roll up the leaves and wrap the ends under. Place them in a shallow baking dish in one layer. Mix the olive oil with enough water to cover the rolled leaves and bake in a preheated 350° oven for about 20 minutes, until the rice is tender. Serve cold.

Quiches, Pâtés, and Mousses

Artichoke Heart and Feta Cheese Quiche

PIRET'S, SAN DIEGO   *Serves 6 to 8*

This slightly salty, tongue-tingling quiche makes an excellent appetizer, sharpening the taste buds as it does.

1 cup cubed or crumbled feta cheese

½ cup chopped red onion, sautéed in a small amount of vegetable oil

1 10-ounce can artichoke hearts, drained, rinsed, and chopped

Salt and pepper to taste

1 tablespoon oregano (or to taste)

1½ tablespoons rosemary (or to taste)

½ cup pitted black olives, chopped

Grated Parmesan cheese (for topping)

4 eggs

3 tablespoons all-purpose flour

1 tablespoon salt

½ teaspoon white pepper

Pinch of nutmeg

1 cup light cream

1 cup milk

In the bottom of an 11-inch pastry-lined (see the *pâte brisée* recipe under Piret's rarebit quiche, page 23) quiche pan, sprinkle the feta cheese.

In a bowl, combine the chopped onion, artichoke hearts, salt, pepper, herbs, and chopped olives. Sprinkle these ingredients on top of the feta cheese and top with the grated Parmesan. Prepare the custard with the remaining ingredients and pour it over all. Bake in a preheated 375° oven until the custard sets, about 45 minutes.

Lox and Onion Quiche

ZABAR'S, NEW YORK CITY (UPPER WEST SIDE)

Serves 4 as a main dish, 8 as an appetizer

Zabar's is a delicatessen *par excellence*, fragrant with pickles and olives, smoked fish and sausages, cheeses and coffees from around the world. On Saturday and Sunday mornings, it is so crowded it can be hard to get through the door. Though Zabar's is famous for all its gustatory delights, its Nova Scotia smoked salmon has the reputation of being the best in the city. Taking advantage of that reputation, Zabar's has started making lox and onion quiches.

1 pound onions, minced
4 tablespoons butter
1 tablespoon flour
2 eggs
Salt and freshly ground black
pepper to taste

Pinch of nutmeg
⅔ cup heavy cream
⅛ pound lox, diced
½ cup grated Swiss cheese
8-inch pie shell, partially baked

Preheat the oven to 375°. In a skillet, over low heat, sauté the onion in 3 tablespoons of butter until the onion is soft and golden. This may take a while, so be patient. Add the flour, stirring it gently, and cook the mixture for 3 minutes. Set aside.

Combine the eggs, salt, pepper, nutmeg, and cream and beat them well. Add the lox, sautéed onion, and half the cheese and mix until blended. Pour the mixture into the pie shell. Sprinkle it with the remaining cheese and dot it with the remaining tablespoon of butter.

Place the quiche pan on a cookie sheet and bake it for 25 to 30 minutes, or until it is brown and puffed up.

Tomato and Dill Quiche

Serves 8 to 10

GOODIES TO GO, LEXINGTON, MASSACHUSETTS

There's a sophistication to the combination of flavors in this quiche that makes it a fine company dish.

Crust

6 tablespoons butter
2 tablespoons shortening or
   lard

1¼ cups all-purpose flour
¼ teaspoon salt
3 to 4 tablespoons ice water

Break the butter and lard into bits. Gradually work it into the combined flour and salt until the mixture reaches the consistency of cornmeal. Make a well in the center and add the ice water a tablespoon at a time until the dough holds together in a ball. Push with the palm of your hand, re-form, push again, and rest and chill the dough for 1 hour.

Roll out the dough and line a 9-inch pie pan. Line the crust with aluminum foil, and fill with 1 cup of dried beans to hold the crust down. Bake for 8 to 10 minutes in a preheated 350° oven.

Filling

1 onion, sliced
3 tablespoons butter
4 eggs
2 cups light cream
Salt and freshly ground black
   pepper to taste

1 tablespoon chopped dill
1 cup grated Gruyère cheese
¼ cup grated Parmesan cheese
1 large tomato, thinly sliced

22

Sauté the onions in the butter until translucent. Mix together the eggs, cream, salt, pepper, and dill. Place the onions in the bottom of the pastry-lined pan. Sprinkle the cheeses on top of the onions and arrange the tomato slices on top. Pour the mixture of eggs, cream, and dill over all. Bake for 30 to 35 minutes in a preheated 375° oven, until the quiche is golden brown and the custard is firm.

Rarebit Quiche

Serves 6 to 8

PIRET'S, SAN DIEGO

In 1975 Piret and George Munger opened The Perfect Pan in San Diego, a store specializing in fine cookware. Two months later, they added a cooking school and a little after that a restaurant serving luncheon. When they began selling gourmet take-out items — *charcuterie* and George's own creations — they had to open a second store. Quiches are among their most popular specialties.

Basic Pâte Brisée (for an 11-inch quiche pan)

1 cup all-purpose flour
1½ sticks butter, very cold or
   frozen, cut into bits

¼ teaspoon salt
½ tablespoon sugar
⅓ cup cold water

Crumble the dry ingredients and the cold butter with your fingertips until the mixture resembles small pebbles. Slowly add the water to bind. Form into a ball and refrigerate the dough before rolling it out. (A food processor can, of course, be used for the mixing process.)

Filling

3 tablespoons flour
1½ tablespoons dry mustard
1 tablespoon paprika
Pinch cayenne pepper and salt
⅓ cup Worcestershire sauce
4 eggs
1½ cups light cream

1½ cups milk
2 handfuls French-style bread
  (cut into ½-inch cubes)
6 ounces grated Cheddar
  cheese
½ cup crumbled cooked bacon
2 tablespoons chopped onion

In a bowl, combine the flour, dry mustard, paprika, cayenne, salt, and Worcestershire sauce. Add the eggs, cream, and milk. Soak the cubes of French bread in the custard for 15 minutes, until they are soft. Drain, reserving the custard.

Line an 11-inch greased quiche pan with the *pâte brisée.* Sprinkle the dough with the grated Cheddar and bacon. Top with the soaked bread cubes and chopped onion. Fill with the custard and bake in a preheated 375° oven until the custard sets, about 45 minutes.

Herb and Three-Cheese Quiche   Serves 6 to 8
PIRET'S, SAN DIEGO

This is a perfect quiche for the buffet or cocktail table.

½ pound cream cheese
3 tablespoons all-purpose flour
4 eggs
½ cup sour cream
Salt and pepper to taste
1 cup milk
1 cup light cream

4 ounces Swiss cheese, grated
1 bunch chives, chopped
½ cup chopped parsley
½ cup chopped scallions
3 tablespoons grated Parmesan
  cheese

24

In a mixing bowl blend the cream cheese, flour, eggs, sour cream, salt, pepper, milk, and cream. Set aside.

Sprinkle the Swiss cheese in a pastry-lined (see the *pâte brisée* recipe under Piret's rarebit quiche, page 23) 11-inch quiche pan. Add the chopped herbs and Parmesan cheese. Fill with the custard mixture and bake in a preheated 375° oven until the custard sets, about 45 minutes.

Providence Cheese Quiche   *Serves 4*

THE PROVIDENCE CHEESE—TAVOLA CALDA,
    PROVIDENCE, RHODE ISLAND

At Providence Cheese on Federal Hill, Providence's Little Italy, they not only sell nearly three hundred kinds of cheese, but they make their own mozzarella, ricotta, and farmer cheese. Owner Frank Basso's crustless quiche uses the ricotta.

1½ pounds fresh, well-drained ricotta
4 eggs, well beaten
Salt and freshly ground black pepper to taste

2 tablespoons grated Parmesan cheese
2 cups chopped raw spinach
Freshly grated bread crumbs

Preheat the oven to 350°. Beat the ricotta and the eggs until the mixture is creamy and light in color. Add the salt and pepper, Parmesan, and spinach. Blend well and pour the mixture into a lightly oiled 8-by-8-by-2-inch pan. Sprinkle the top lightly with grated bread crumbs and bake for 15 minutes, until golden. If you prefer raw zucchini to spinach, it also works well in this quiche.

Torta Rustica

Serves 6

SUZANNE'S, WASHINGTON, D.C.

Although relatively new to Washington, gourmet take-out food shops are a natural in that city, with its population of young single professionals. Some of Suzanne's customers come by almost daily to select their dinners from the cases in this long, narrow shop with tiled floors and white stucco walls. Suzanne suggests this *torta rustica* for a picnic. It would be equally good on a buffet table or for lunch, served with a salad.

Brioche Dough

2 tablespoons active dry yeast
¼ cup warm water
1 to 1½ cups all-purpose flour
1 tablespoon sugar

1 teaspoon salt
2 eggs plus 1 egg yolk
½ cup softened butter

Filling

2 tablespoons oil
1 green pepper, thinly sliced
1 red pepper, thinly sliced
1 small yellow onion, thinly sliced
½ pound soprasatta or Genoa salami
1 pound ricotta
1 teaspoon crushed fennel seeds

1 tablespoon chopped fresh basil (or 1 teaspoon dried)
½ cup chopped parsley
4 eggs, lightly beaten
Salt and freshly ground black pepper to taste
2 cups grated Asiago or Romano cheese

Dissolve the yeast in the warm water. Mix the flour (use 1 cup at first, but add the remaining ½ cup if necessary), sugar, salt, and eggs until smooth. Stir in the yeast mixture. Beat in the butter a tablespoon at a time. Knead the dough and let it rise for 1 hour, or until it has doubled in bulk. Punch it down and let it rest for a few minutes. Knead again, adding more flour if necessary. The dough should be fairly stiff.

26

On a heavily floured surface, roll out two 12-inch circles. Be sure the dough is thin. Place one circle on the bottom of a buttered 12-inch pie pan or pizza pan. Pull the dough up over the sides of the pan.

Heat the oil in a frying pan and sauté the peppers and onions until they are soft. Set aside.

Cut the salami into julienne strips and combine it with the ricotta, herbs, eggs, salt, pepper, and 1 cup of the grated cheese.

Sprinkle the other cup of grated cheese over the brioche dough in the pan. Alternate layers of the sautéed vegetable mixture with the ricotta mixture, ending with the ricotta.

Place the second brioche circle over the top of the *torta* and pinch the top and bottom edges together to seal the dough.

Brush the top with a mixture of one egg and 1 tablespoon water and bake the *torta rustica* in a preheated 400° oven for 30 minutes. Turn the heat down to 350° and bake for another 30 minutes, or until the top is golden and the filling firm. Cool completely before cutting.

Crab Roulade
Serves 8

SUTTON PLACE GOURMET, WASHINGTON, D.C.

Everything's big at Sutton Place Gourmet, from the size of the store to the names of its patrons. With 10,000 square feet of selling space, it claims to be the largest gourmet food shop in the world, and it is certainly the only one where you could find yourself on the check-out line with the vice president, the secretary of state, or Ethel Kennedy, who, according to owner Jeffrey Cohen, buys "very expensive prepared frozen food and tons of candy." One of the take-out dishes big with the Sutton Place clientele is this crab *roulade*.

1 pound lump crab meat (preferably back-fin crab, if available)

12 ounces fresh spinach or 1 10-ounce package frozen chopped spinach (thawed)

1 pound ricotta

2 tablespoons ground coriander

1 teaspoon salt

1 teaspoon freshly ground white pepper

1 1-pound package frozen phyllo pastry sheets, thawed

Melted butter (about ½ cup)

Carefully pick over the crab meat and put the pieces in a large bowl.

If you are using fresh spinach, wash it well and steam it briefly. Drain and chop it. Wrap it in the corner of a towel and squeeze out all the moisture. Frozen spinach need not be cooked, but it must be squeezed in a towel after it has thawed.

Add the spinach, ricotta, and seasonings to the crab meat and mix together. The mixture will be quite firm. Put the bowl in the refrigerator while you prepare the phyllo pastry.

Using a wax-paper surface and starting at the edge nearest you: Lay out one sheet of the pastry lengthwise across the bottom of the surface. Brush it with melted butter. Place the second sheet of pastry over the first, leaving 1 inch of the first sheet nearest to you uncovered. Brush with melted butter.

Continue in the same manner, always leaving the nearest 1 inch of the next-to-the-top layer uncovered. You may use as few as five sheets to make your pastry rectangle, but ten sheets will give you a nice crusty *roulade*.

After you have brushed the last sheet with melted butter, spread the crab filling across the bottom of the rectangle and roll up the pastry.

Place the *roulade* in a buttered baking dish and bake it in a preheated 375° oven for 12 to 15 minutes, until it is golden.

Note: Although the *roulade* may be baked in a roll, as described, it is easier to handle and looks prettier if you slice it into pieces before you bake it.

Shrimp Frittata *Serves 3 or 4*
E.A.T., NEW YORK CITY (UPPER EAST SIDE)

There are now two E.A.T.s on Madison Avenue, the newer one a smashing establishment in the old Rhinelander mansion, a French Renaissance château at the corner of Seventy-second Street. *The New Yorker* described it as "a handsome shop, filled with light, food, and rich people." Omnipresent in the shop is Eli Zabar, seasoning salads, superintending the hand-dipping of strawberries and apricots into melted chocolate, or checking this shrimp *frittata* for garlic.

3 tablespoons butter	¼ cup heavy cream
8 cloves garlic (or to taste)	¼ pound butter, melted
½ pound cooked shrimp	Salt and freshly ground black
6 eggs	pepper to taste

Melt the 3 tablespoons of butter in a saucepan and add the garlic and shrimp. Cover the pan and steam for 8 to 10 minutes over low heat, until the garlic is soft but not brown.

Lightly beat the eggs, add the cream and melted butter, and stir in the garlic and shrimp. Season with salt and pepper. Pour the mixture into a buttered 8-inch cast-iron pan or oven-proof skillet. Bake in a preheated 400° oven for 10 to 15 minutes, or until firm. Let the *frittata* cool for a few minutes before serving, until it pulls away from the sides of the pan.

French Onion Tart

THE CHARCUTERIE, WELLESLEY, MASSACHUSETTS

The marvelous window display — giant papier-mâché vegetables tumbling out of a huge brown paper bag — that introduces customers to The Charcuterie is the work of Kim Sammis, set designer for the Boston Children's Theatre. This onion tart is one of the specialties of chef Nancy Hodgson.

Pie Crust

½ teaspoon active dry yeast
½ cup lukewarm water
1 teaspoon salt

1½ cups all-purpose flour
1 teaspoon olive oil

Filling

1 pound Spanish onions, chopped
½ cup olive oil
2 teaspoons Dijon mustard, preferably with seeds
¼ pound Gruyère cheese, grated

3 or 4 ripe tomatoes
¼ pound Niçoise or other black olives, pitted
1 teaspoon dried basil
Freshly ground black pepper

Dissolve the yeast in the lukewarm water in a large bowl. Set it aside for 2 to 3 minutes to let the yeast activate. Mix the salt with the flour and add with the olive oil to the yeast mixture. Mix thoroughly and turn the dough out onto a floured surface. Knead it for 10 minutes. Rub a large bowl with oil and put the ball of dough in it. Turn it over once to coat it with the oil. Cover the bowl with a towel and put it in a warm place until doubled in bulk, 1½ to 2 hours.

Sauté the onions in ⅓ cup of the olive oil. Cook them slowly over medium heat until they are quite brown, but not burned. This will bring out the sweetness of the onions. Let cool.

Punch down the dough and roll it into a circle to fit a 9-inch tart pan. Spread the mustard over the dough and top it with the onions and the grated cheese.

Core and halve the tomatoes and cut each half into six pieces. Arrange the pieces in concentric circles on the tart and fill in the spaces with the black olives. Sprinkle with basil and pepper. Spoon the remaining olive oil over all.

Set the tart in a warm spot until the dough has risen slightly over the edge of the pan. Bake the tart in a preheated 375° oven for 30 to 35 minutes. Serve warm or at room temperature. To reheat the tart, place it on a cookie sheet and warm it in a 275° oven for about 20 minutes.

Chicken Liver Pâté

Serves 15 to 20

REX'S MARKET DELICATESSEN, SEATTLE

When you want something a bit less rich than Formaggio Kitchen's chicken liver mousse (page 33), try this very good pâté.

⅓ pound butter
¾ cup chopped onions
2 pounds chicken livers, trimmed of fat
¾ cup dry sherry
1 teaspoon salt, or to taste

½ teaspoon freshly ground white pepper
1 teaspoon mace
½ teaspoon nutmeg
½ teaspoon coriander

Sauté the onions in the butter for 5 minutes. Add the livers and cook for an additional 5 minutes over moderate heat. Add the remaining ingredients and cook for 5 minutes longer. Force the mixture through a sieve or purée it in a food processor. Put it into the dish from which it will be served. Chill until set.

Hunter's Pâté

Serves 20

THE FRUIT LADY, PHILADELPHIA

Between the fruits and vegetables attractively displayed at the back of the store and the ninety-six varieties of cheeses (and other specialty items) in front is a glass display counter filled with tempting carry-out foods, including this pâté.

¼ pound butter
2 cloves garlic
2 large onions, chopped
5 red Delicious apples, peeled and roughly chopped
1 tablespoon basil
1 tablespoon thyme
3 pounds chicken livers

1 cup brandy
3 bay leaves
5 egg yolks
5 tablespoons flour
½ cup heavy cream
5 tablespoons sugar
Salt and freshly ground black pepper to taste

In a large saucepan, melt the butter and sauté the garlic, onions, and apples. Add the basil and thyme and cook until the ingredients are soft. Add the livers and cook until the outsides change color but the insides are still pink. Add the brandy and cook for 3 to 5 minutes to allow the alcohol to burn off. Purée the mixture through a food mill and set aside.

Beat together the egg yolks, flour, and cream, and add it to the pâté mixture. Stir in the sugar, salt, and pepper. Put the pâté in a 2-quart oven-proof crock, cover the crock with foil, and set it in a baking dish. Fill the baking dish with water about 2 inches deep. Bake in a preheated 375° oven for 45 minutes.

Cool.

Chicken Liver Mousse

FORMAGGIO KITCHEN, CAMBRIDGE

What do a Nobel Prize winner, the publisher of the *New Republic*, a Rockefeller, the author of *The Hotel New Hampshire*, and a food writer for the *Boston Globe* have in common? For one thing, they all patronize Formaggio Kitchen, an establishment that also has the reputation, according to owner Norma Wasserman, of feeding half the bachelors in Cambridge.

This is a truly elegant mousse, meltingly smooth and simultaneously rich and light. The raisins are an unusual addition.

1 pound chicken livers
⅓ pound butter, clarified
1 medium onion, chopped
2 or 3 cloves garlic, chopped
A generous pinch of thyme,
    allspice, cloves, ginger, and
    coriander

1 bay leaf
3 tablespoons cognac
¼ cup dry sherry
1 pound butter, softened
Salt and freshly ground black
    pepper to taste
Chopped raisins (for garnish)

Remove the veins from the livers and pat them dry. Sauté the livers in the clarified butter over medium-high heat, tossing them frequently so they don't stick to the pan. Cook until they are just firm (still slightly pink inside) and remove them from the pan.

Put the onions, garlic, and spices into the same pan and cook over low heat until the onions are translucent. Remove the bay leaf. Add this mixture to the livers.

Still using the same pan, pour in the cognac and put the pan back on the burner to ignite the cognac. Turn off the heat and stir the juices until the flame goes out. (If you have an electric stove, you may have to ignite the cognac with a match instead of the flame.) Add the sherry, and simmer, scraping the residue from the bottom of the pan, until the liquid is reduced by half. Pour it over the livers and let them cool completely.

Cream the butter.

In a food processor, slowly combine equal parts of butter and the liver mixture in batches. Blend until very smooth. Season to taste with salt and pepper.

Spread the mousse into a serving bowl and garnish with chopped raisins. Serve with Melba toast or crackers.

Green Peppercorn Terrine
GRETCHEN'S OF COURSE, SEATTLE

Makes two pâtés, about 2 pounds each

This terrine improves if it is allowed to season for a day or two in the refrigerator. And since the ingredients should be marinated overnight, too, before you start working with them, allow plenty of time for preparation.

2½ pounds ground pork
1½ pounds ground veal
⅔ pound ground ham
1 pound ground pork fat
1 medium onion, finely chopped
4 cloves garlic, minced or mashed
2 teaspoons thyme
2 teaspoons allspice

2 teaspoons salt
2 tablespoons coarsely ground black pepper
¾ cup brandy
4 to 6 ounces green peppercorns
4 eggs, lightly beaten
1½ pounds thinly sliced fatback

The ground meats and pork fat should be of medium texture. Mix them together and mix in the onion, garlic, thyme, allspice, salt, pepper, brandy, and green peppercorns. Cover, and refrigerate

34

overnight to marinate for best flavor. The following day, mix in the eggs until completely blended. Line two 9-by-5-inch loaf pans with the fatback in such a way that the slices extend beyond the pan rims by 2 to 3 inches on all sides. Pack in the meat mixture, pressing to eliminate air pockets. Fold over the fatback to cover the meat completely. Cover each pan snugly with two layers of aluminum foil; crimp it around the edges to make a tight seal.

Bake the terrines in a water bath in a preheated 325° oven for 3 hours, or until the juices run clear when the pâté is pressed. Remove the pans from the oven and the water bath. Place weights — wrapped bricks or heavy cans — on each pâté and cool.

When cool, remove the weights and refrigerate for at least 24 hours before serving. To serve, unmold and scrape all but a thin layer of the fat from the surface. Slice thinly.

Mousse de Poisson   *Serves 10 to 20*
LA BELLE CUISINE, GLENCOE, ILLINOIS

This trout mousse is most delicious in its own right, but if you wish an extra fillip, a cup of shrimp, bay scallops, fresh salmon, or vegetables may be added for a variation in flavor and color.

2 pounds fresh lake trout fillets, skinned and cut into ½-pound pieces
4 eggs, separated
2 tablespoons unflavored gelatin
1 teaspoon salt
¼ teaspoon freshly ground white pepper
2 cups whipping cream

In a food processor, process the fillets for 30 seconds. Add the egg yolks, gelatin, salt, pepper, and 1 cup of the cream. Process for 30 seconds.

35

Whip the second cup of cream until it is stiff. Whip the egg whites until they are stiff but not dry. Fold together the fish mixture, the whipped cream, and the whipped egg whites.

Pour the mixture into a greased 8-cup loaf pan. Cover it with buttered aluminum foil or parchment paper. Place it in a *bain-marie* with the water reaching halfway up the loaf pan's sides and bake it for 45 minutes at 350°. Cool it overnight.

To unmold the mousse, put the loaf pan in hot water for a minute or two; then invert it onto a platter and slice. Serve the mousse cold with homemade mayonnaise.

Fish Pâté   Serves 15 to 20

BAGATELLE, BEVERLY HILLS

When André Pister was a chef at Le Bonne Auberge in Antibes, King Farouk, King Baudouin, and Cary Grant were among his customers. Now he has his own gourmet take-out shop and French restaurant in Beverly Hills, and Orson Welles, Walter Pidgeon, and Vincent Price are part of his clientele. His layered fish pâté looks as good as it tastes.

2½ pounds fresh salmon
1 pound scallops
1 pound shrimp, peeled and deveined
Salt and freshly ground black pepper to taste
½ cup cognac
1 cup heavy cream

2 whole eggs plus 2 egg whites, lightly beaten together
1 teaspoon green peppercorns
Cayenne to taste
1 tablespoon truffles (optional)
2 pounds fillet of sole

36

In a meat grinder or food processor, grind 2 pounds of the salmon very fine with half the scallops and half the shrimp. Add salt and pepper, half the cognac, half the cream, half the egg mixture, half the green peppercorns, a pinch or so of cayenne, and half the truffles. Blend until smooth. Set aside.

Again using a meat grinder or food processor, grind the sole with the remaining scallops and shrimp. Again add salt, pepper, and cayenne, as well as the remaining cognac, cream, egg mixture, green peppercorns, and truffles. Blend until smooth.

Grease two 8-by-3½-inch loaf pans (preferably Pyrex) and line them with wax paper. Into each loaf pan spoon a layer of the salmon mixture and smooth it; then spoon in a layer of the sole mixture and smooth it. Take the remaining unground salmon and, in finger-sized strips, lay it on top of the sole mixture. Top this with more sole mixture, then more salmon mixture.

Preheat the oven to 350°. Place the loaf pans in a baking dish and pour enough water into the baking dish to reach halfway up the sides of the loaf pans. Cover the pâtés with wax paper and cook until a table knife slipped into the center comes out clean — approximately 2 hours. Cool the pâtés. Serve in thin slices with mustard sauce and sliced lemon on the side.

Scallop Mousse   *Serves 8*

LES TROIS PETITS COCHONS CHARCUTERIE,
NEW YORK CITY (EAST SIDE)

Eighteen different homemade pâtés, plus *boudins, rillettes, andouillettes*, and garlic sausage, are among the specialties of "The Three Little Pigs," which markets its pâtés in every state in the Union. Mousses, too, are popular with its customers.

This one is a delightful summer treat eaten cold with mayonnaise, or it may be served hot with *beurre d'échalote* or a lobster sauce. For best results in preparing this recipe use very, very cold ingredients.

1½ pounds scallops
3 small shallots, chopped
½ to 1 clove garlic (optional), chopped
1 tablespoon salt
Pinch of freshly ground white pepper

Small pinch of nutmeg
3 tablespoons cognac
Pinch of saffron
1 bunch parsley
3 eggs
3 cups heavy cream, chilled
1 tablespoon tomato paste

Combine the scallops, shallots, garlic, salt, pepper, and nutmeg, and divide the mixture into three parts. Wrap each section in plastic wrap and chill in the freezer. Heat 1 tablespoon of the cognac with the saffron and chill it in the refrigerator. Boil 2 cups of water with 2 tablespoons of salt and blanch the parsley in the water for 2 to 3 minutes. Drain it and run it under cold water. Press out any excess water and put the parsley in the refrigerator. (Spinach, chives, or any other green may be substituted for the parsley.)

Using a food processor, process one of the three portions of scallops for a minute or two. While the processor is running, add one of the three eggs and mix. Then add 1 tablespoon of cognac and mix well. Next add 1 cup of the chilled cream and process until it is completely mixed. Scrape this mixture from the container into a bowl and put it in the refrigerator.

For the second layer, repeat the above process, but add the blanched parsley at the beginning with the scallop mixture.

For the third layer, again repeat the first procedure, but add the tomato paste at the beginning with the scallop mixture and add the cognac and saffron infusion before the cream.

Brush the insides of a rectangular 8-by-4-by-3½-inch bread pan or terrine with melted butter. Pour the three mixtures into the pan, alternating the colors and evening out the layers with a spatula. Bake the mousse, covered with aluminum foil, in a preheated 250° oven for 2½ hours. Chill, unmold, and serve.

Smoked Salmon Mousse   *Serves 10*
SUTTON PLACE GOURMET, WASHINGTON, D.C.

With a brashness that matches his claim to run "the nation's largest and finest one-stop gourmet department store," Jeffrey Cohen compares his epicurean extravaganza to Fauchon in Paris and Fortnum and Mason in London. Worldwide superlatives aside, Sutton Place Gourmet is certainly the hottest new grocery store in Washington.

Chef Peter Watts's recipe for smoked salmon mousse is one of the best versions of this popular cocktail accompaniment.

1 cup heavy cream
¼ pound smoked salmon
8 ounces cream cheese, softened
1 tablespoon Hungarian paprika
½ teaspoon freshly ground white pepper

1 tablespoon chopped fresh dill
1 tablespoon unflavored gelatin
Juice of 2 lemons plus enough white wine to equal 1 cup of liquid
½ cup mayonnaise

Whip the cream until it makes soft peaks. Refrigerate until needed.

Finely chop the smoked salmon and mix it with the softened cream cheese. (If you use a food processor, don't soften the cream cheese before blending.) Mix in the paprika, pepper, and dill. Set aside.

Stir the gelatin into the lemon juice and wine. Let it soak for 3 minutes, then heat the liquid over medium heat until it clears, but don't let it boil. Allow it to cool, then fold in the mayonnaise.

Fold the mayonnaise mixture into the cream cheese and smoked salmon mixture, then fold in the whipped cream. Pour the mousse into a bowl or individual ramekins. Chill for at least 1 hour, until the mousse is set. Serve with crackers.

Smoked Trout Mousse
Makes 3 cups

THE CHEF'S GARDEN AND TRUFFLES, NAPLES, FLORIDA

This mousse is easy to make and, served with well-buttered Melba toast, is an inviting appetizer, indeed. It is ever popular at both The Chef's Garden restaurant downstairs and the Truffles café and take-out upstairs.

2 8-ounce smoked trout
2 tablespoons chopped
   scallions
½ teaspoon salt
½ teaspoon freshly ground
   white pepper

⅛ teaspoon nutmeg
2 teaspoons chopped fresh dill
1 tablespoon unflavored gelatin
2 cups heavy cream

Skin and bone the trout and purée it in a food processor with the scallions and the seasonings.

Dissolve the gelatin in the cream. Heat it to ensure that the graininess is gone. Add the cream to the trout mixture and process it for 5 to 6 seconds. Pour it into a 3-cup mold.

Chill the mousse for at least 6 hours before unmolding and serving it.

Soups and Chowders

Spinach and Egg Drop Soup

Serves 5 or 6

ABBONDANZA, NEW YORK CITY (UPPER EAST SIDE)

Although Lou Galterio thought he was opening a convenient neighborhood place where customers could buy restaurant-quality Italian food, Abbondanza was scarcely open before people started flocking to it from all parts of the city. The café–take-out shop is stunning, and the variety of foods, according to the *New York Times*, is unmatched by any other store in the city. With its cluster of café tables just inside the door, the atmosphere is Via Veneto, not Second Avenue.

This light and nourishing soup is one of Sicilian-born chef Giuseppe Allegra's favorite recipes. Its Italian name is *stracciatella*, or "torn curtains," so named for the way the eggs and cheese look in the soup.

1 pound spinach
½ cup grated Parmesan cheese
5 beaten eggs

3 quarts chicken or veal stock, or undiluted canned chicken broth
Salt and freshly ground black pepper to taste

Cook the spinach and drain and chop it. Beat the cheese into the eggs.

Bring the stock to a boil and drop the spinach into it. Cook it for 1 to 2 minutes, then add the beaten eggs and cheese. Turn the heat up and boil the stock for 1 minute. As soon as the eggs and cheese form threads, turn off the heat. Taste for seasonings and adjust if necessary. Serve immediately.

42

Split Pea Soup Jardinière

THE FRUIT LADY, PHILADELPHIA

The Fruit Lady is actually two ladies, Joan Arensberg and Phyllis Brodsky, and their shop in the Rittenhouse Square area sells considerably more than fruit. At one end of the prepared food counter is a container of steaming hot, freshly made soup, ready to go. This is one of their best.

5 leeks, cleaned and diced
5 carrots, scraped and diced
5 stalks celery, diced
5 tablespoons butter
2½ cups split peas
4 quarts chicken stock or canned chicken broth

1 bouquet garni
5 tablespoons oil
5 tablespoons flour
½ pound cooked ham, cubed
2½ cups heavy cream
Salt and freshly ground black pepper to taste

In a large stockpot, sauté the leeks, carrots, and celery in the butter for 4 minutes. Add the split peas and the chicken stock and bring to a boil. Add the bouquet garni, reduce the heat, cover, and simmer for 2 hours, stirring occasionally.

In a small saucepan, stir the oil and flour together and cook until tan. Add a little of the soup and whisk until the mixture is smooth. Whisk the thickening mixture into the soup, a little at a time, until it is all incorporated.

Add the ham and the heavy cream. Season to taste with salt and pepper.

Lentil Soup

Serves 6 to 8

THE CHAPLAIN'S PANTRY, TACOMA, WASHINGTON

In addition to the fine wines, rare cooking equipment, and gourmet specialties sold at the Reverend Jeffrey Smith's "Pantry," some of the dishes from his restaurant — the Chaplain's Judicial Annex — are put up to take out. The restaurant, which caters to a mix of law students and business professionals, offers generous entrées, old-fashioned sodas, espresso, and spirits. And for a student losing his current case or taking a course from a dreaded professor, Mr. Smith points out that each chair has its own prayer kneeler. Hot soup is helpful, too.

2 cups dry lentils
1 quart water
2 quarts brown beef stock, or canned beef broth
1 potato, diced
1 carrot, grated

3 tablespoons white vinegar
Salt to taste (not too much)
2 teaspoons ground cloves
Dry sherry
Romano or Parmesan cheese, grated

In a soup pot, soak the lentils for 2 hours in the water. Add the stock, potato, carrot, vinegar, salt, and cloves and cook over low heat for 3 hours. To serve, put a splash of sherry in each individual soup bowl. Add the soup and garnish with grated cheese.

Cream of Broccoli Soup

Serves 8

THE AMERICAN CAFÉ MARKET, WASHINGTON, D.C.

This superb broccoli soup is sold to be eaten hot, but it is really just as good cold. The barely cooked broccoli flowerets, the lemon zest, and the watercress leaves give it a crisp, tangy taste and texture.

1 small onion
1 medium leek
1½ heads broccoli
2 stalks celery
1½ cups sliced mushrooms
6 tablespoons butter
2 tablespoons flour
5 cups chicken stock (or three 13¾-ounce cans of chicken broth)

½ to 1 tablespoon salt, depending on how salty the chicken stock is
¼ teaspoon freshly ground black pepper
Pinch of nutmeg
¾ cup milk
1 cup heavy cream
Grated zest of 1 lemon
1 cup watercress leaves, loosely packed

Chop the onion and the well-washed leek. Separate the broccoli flowerets from the stems and set aside. Shred the broccoli stems and the celery in a food processor.

Heat the butter in a large pot and add the onions, leeks, broccoli stems, celery, and mushrooms. Sauté for 7 minutes and then sprinkle with the flour. Sauté for 3 minutes longer.

Add the chicken stock, salt, pepper, nutmeg, and milk, and simmer for 25 minutes.

Purée the soup in a blender or food processor until it is smooth. Return the soup to the stove and add the cream, broccoli flowerets, and lemon zest. Simmer for 7 minutes and taste for salt and pepper. Pour the soup into bowls and garnish with the watercress leaves.

Note: If you reheat the soup, don't let it overcook, or the broccoli flowerets will lose their crisp texture.

Cream of Asparagus and Morel Soup   *Serves 8*
LA BELLE CUISINE, GLENCOE, ILLINOIS

In the spring, fresh morels are available in such northern states as Michigan and Wisconsin, either for your own picking (if you know what to look for) or in markets for $10 or so a pound. Dried morels, which must be reconstituted before cooking, can be bought in gourmet groceries. Or you can substitute ordinary white mushrooms in this soup. The flavor won't be quite so elegant, but almost.

1 pound fresh asparagus, cut in 1-inch pieces

½ pound fresh morels, chopped or sliced (or 1 pound fresh mushrooms, sliced)

4 tablespoons finely chopped shallots

4 tablespoons butter

1 teaspoon lemon juice

3 cups rich chicken stock

1 cup heavy cream

Salt and freshly ground black pepper to taste

A roux made of 2 tablespoons butter and 2 tablespoons flour

Cook the asparagus until quite tender, and purée it in a food processor. Lightly sauté the morels (or mushrooms) and shallots in the butter. Add the lemon juice and asparagus purée and sauté for 1 minute more. Gradually add the chicken stock. Add the cream and salt and pepper. Add the roux in small amounts, and bring the soup just to a boil. Serve immediately.

Cream of Carrot with Dill Soup   *Serves 10 to 12*

GOODIES TO GO, LEXINGTON, MASSACHUSETTS

Gaye Pickrel of Goodies feels that tired and hungry commuters need tempting, nourishing food at the end of a long day. So she prepares dishes that "look beautiful and taste good" in her attractive, brick-walled shop that is filled with the fragrances of baked goods and spices and a wood-burning stove.

1½ quarts chicken broth
1 to 1½ pounds carrots, peeled and chopped
2 large onions, chopped
Salt and freshly ground black pepper to taste

1 cup sour cream
½ bunch fresh dill, finely chopped
Cream or milk to thin out

Bring the chicken broth to a steady simmer and add the carrots, onions, salt, and pepper. Simmer for 20 to 25 minutes, until the vegetables are soft. Remove from the heat and purée the broth and the vegetables using a food mill or a blender. Add the sour cream. Transfer the soup to a larger pot and add the dill. Add enough cream or milk to achieve the consistency you desire. For a flavorful change, substitute tarragon or curry for the dill in the soup.

Milanese Pesto Soup

THE FRUIT LADY, PHILADELPHIA

A great soup anytime, but especially nice to make when your garden is producing. The pesto may be fresh or frozen, and any version will do. There's a good one on page 176.

4 cups chopped onions
1 bunch celery, chopped
1 pound carrots, chopped
½ cup butter
3 quarts chicken stock or canned chicken broth
5 zucchini, sliced

4 or 5 tomatoes, peeled, seeded, and chopped
Salt and freshly ground black pepper to taste
½ cup pesto
¼ cup grated Parmesan cheese

Sauté the onions, celery, and carrots in the butter in a large pot. Add the chicken stock and simmer until the vegetables are almost tender. Don't overcook. Add the zucchini, tomatoes, salt, and pepper, and cook until all the vegetables are just tender. Stir in the pesto and Parmesan cheese. Correct the seasonings. Serve.

Potage Provençal

Serves 15

THE PUBLIC COOKSHOP, PHILADELPHIA

"We give discounts to customers who throw away their pots and pans," jokes Deborah Baldwin, co-owner with Kirk Rynearson of this Center City shop that sells nothing but freshly prepared foods made in its own kitchen — no groceries, no cheeses, no frozen foods, and no restaurant.

With its forty selections available every day, The Public Cookshop is an alternative for people who want to eat at home without grocery shopping or cooking. For those who haven't thrown out the stockpot, this is a delicious, hearty soup.

5 cups white beans	3 cloves garlic, minced
1 pound bacon, chopped	3 bay leaves
1 large onion, chopped	2 teaspoons thyme
2 cups dry white wine	2 teaspoons rosemary
2 cups Italian plum tomatoes, fresh or canned	Salt and freshly ground black pepper to taste
2½ to 3 quarts chicken stock	

Soak the beans in water overnight. Drain and set aside.

Brown the bacon in a large stockpot. Drain off all but 3 tablespoons of the fat and sauté the onion in it. Add all the remaining ingredients and the beans and simmer for 2 hours.

Purée half of this mixture and return it to the pot. If it is too thick, add more chicken stock. Simmer for an additional 30 minutes. Correct the seasoning.

Corn Chowder

PROOF OF THE PUDDING, ATLANTA

Although this is a year-round chowder, it is especially good in the summertime, when it can be made with fresh sweet corn. With crusty French bread or a light sandwich, it is a filling lunch.

1½ cups minced onion
5 tablespoons butter
¼ teaspoon sage
¾ teaspoon whole cumin
¾ teaspoon marjoram
⅓ cup flour
3 cups chicken stock or broth
½ cup Chablis
2 cups heavy cream
½ teaspoon nutmeg

1 chopped green pepper
1 12-ounce can of corn (drained), 1 10-ounce package frozen corn, or 1½ cups fresh corn
6 ounces Cheddar cheese, grated
2 tablespoons chopped parsley
Tabasco and Worcestershire sauce to taste

Sauté the onions in the butter until they are transparent. Add the herbs and stir until they are fragrant. Add the flour and stir, cooking for 2 or 3 minutes over low heat. Add the chicken stock and Chablis and whisk until the liquid thickens. Add the cream, nutmeg, green pepper, and corn and simmer for 10 minutes (or 15 minutes if the corn is fresh). Add the cheese and turn off the heat. Add the parsley, Tabasco, and Worcestershire sauce.

Lobster Bisque *Serves 8*

A MOVEABLE FEAST, PHILADELPHIA

When it's "lobster bisque to go," you know how far the new gourmet take-out food shops are removed from the fried-chicken-in-a-basket emporia. In Philadelphia, as in many cities today, some of the best and most imaginatively prepared food is served in containers, to be taken home and heated up. The owners of this shop have been catering to their well-educated, well-traveled, academic clientele for seven years.

1¼ cups diced carrots
1 small onion
½ pound uncooked lobster or langoustino meat
1 cup butter
2 tablespoons dry sherry
½ cup dry white wine
¾ cup chicken broth

1 tablespoon tomato paste
1 bay leaf
2 tablespoons minced parsley
Pinch of thyme
8 tablespoons flour
4 cups scalded milk
4 tablespoons heavy cream

Mince the carrots and onion in a food processor. Mince the lobster meat.

Melt half the butter in a large pot and sauté the carrots and onions for 5 minutes. Add the lobster meat. Heat and ignite the sherry and pour it over the mixture. Add the wine, chicken broth, tomato paste, bay leaf, parsley, and thyme, and simmer for 20 minutes.

Melt the rest of the butter in a saucepan and stir in the flour to make a roux. Cook it for a few minutes and then add the hot milk, beating vigorously with a wire whisk. Pour this into the lobster pot and simmer very gently for 15 minutes. Add the cream and correct the seasonings.

51

Oyster Stew I

NEUMAN & BOGDONOFF, NEW YORK CITY
(UPPER EAST SIDE)

Paul Neuman and Stacy Bogdonoff learned their business working at the Rosedale Fish Market, a Lexington Avenue shop started by Paul's grandfather seventy-five years ago. To the fresh fish and shellfish the market had always been known for, they introduced their own delicious prepared dishes. Now Paul and Stacy have a separate shop that specializes in their gourmet carry-out items — including this oyster stew, designed to be eaten as a first course.

2 tablespoons butter	1 cup heavy cream
2 leeks (white part only), washed and chopped	Salt, freshly ground black pepper, and nutmeg to taste
24 shucked oysters with 1 quart oyster juice	Chopped parsley (for garnish)

Melt the butter in a saucepan. Add the leeks and cook over medium heat for 2 or 3 minutes, until transparent.

Add the oysters and the oyster juice. Turn the heat up a little and cook for another 2 to 3 minutes, until the edges of the oysters curl. Add the cream and seasonings and heat until the stew is just warmed through. Sprinkle with parsley, and serve.

Oyster Stew II

THE FISHMONGER, CAMBRIDGE

In the all-male world of the Boston fish pier, women are outsiders, not to be taken seriously. When Dorothy Borden, as the new owner of The Fishmonger, tried to find someone to show her how to fillet a fish, she finally had to give up and teach herself from a book. Still, she showed up on the pier each morning and paid her bills promptly, and when the fishermen got together and bought her a pair of heavy rubber boots to replace her running shoes, she knew she had been accepted. Today she continues to buy fish daily; fish that is not sold the day it is bought is cooked up into one of the many prepared dishes the shop sells.

2 pints shucked oysters (about 66 oysters)

4 tablespoons butter

3 large shallots, finely chopped (about ½ cup)

1 bay leaf, broken up

1 cup finely chopped celery

Finely grated rind of 1 lemon

2¼ quarts light cream

1½ teaspoons salt, or to taste

1 teaspoon hot sauce, 4 teaspoons Worcestershire sauce, and ⅓ teaspoon paprika, mixed together

6 tablespoons butter

2 tablespoons finely chopped parsley

Dashes of paprika

Remove any bits of shell from the oysters.

Melt the butter in a pot large enough to hold 3 quarts of liquid. Sauté the shallots with the bay leaf pieces until soft. Add the celery and lemon rind, and sauté until the celery is soft but still slightly firm. Add the cream and salt and heat until the cream is almost scalding.

Add the oysters and cook gently, stirring, for about 3 minutes — until the edges of the oysters start to curl and the bodies offer resistance when touched. Add the hot sauce–Worcestershire–paprika mixture. Stir well and taste for seasoning.

With a slotted spoon, divide the oysters among six warmed serving bowls. Add the liquid and garnish each bowl of stew with a tablespoon of butter, some chopped parsley, and a dash of paprika.

Quahaug Chowder

Serves 9 to 12

POOLE'S FISH MARKET, MENEMSHA, MASSACHUSETTS

Connoisseurs of quahaug chowder swear by the simple version prepared at Poole's Fish Market on Martha's Vineyard. This chowder freezes remarkably well at the stage before the milk is added. On a cold winter's night, simply remove the base from your freezer, add the milk and a dollop of butter, heat, and serve.

1 pint minced quahaug meats
with their liquid
4 potatoes, peeled and sliced
1 large onion

3 tablespoons butter
1½ quarts rich milk
Salt and freshly ground pepper
to taste

Cook the potatoes and quahaugs in enough water to cover just until they are tender. Dice the onion and sauté it in the butter. Add the onion to the potatoes and quahaugs. If you are storing it, cool and freeze the chowder base at this stage. If you are serving it, add the milk, heat, and serve — but do not allow the chowder to boil, or it will curdle. Season with salt and pepper.

Variations that Poole's does not sell call for the substitution of 1 2-inch cube of salt pork for the butter, or half light cream and half milk for the 1½ quarts rich milk.

Fisherman's Stew

Serves 10 to 12

POOLE'S FISH MARKET, MENEMSHA, MASSACHUSETTS

Everett Poole, who loves to eat but hates to cook, collaborated on this recipe with his friend Joe Hyde, a chef and cookbook

54

author. Everett wanted a dish that would take advantage of the large variety of fresh fish that is landed at Menemsha, one that would please both the palate and his New England sense of thrift. Designed to make 500 pints of stew, their recipe begins, "Take 185 pounds of mixed fish . . ." For this book, Poole's manager, Jake Hakes, a former restaurant chef, reduced the recipe to manageable size and adjusted the seasonings for the home kitchen.

4 pounds of mixed fish — use any combination of bluefish, black bass, swordfish, scrod, cod, striped bass, sea bass, eel, or scup (porgy)

Enough fish stock to cover (see recipe below)

2-inch cube of salt pork

1 large or 2 medium onions, diced

3 shallots, diced

3 cloves garlic, minced

3 stalks celery, diced

½ teaspoon Hungarian paprika

2 cups plus 6 tablespoons dry white vermouth

¾ cup tomato purée

Juice of 1 lemon

½ teaspoon thyme

¾ teaspoon tarragon

8 tablespoons cornstarch

¾ cup chopped parsley

1 cup hot milk or light cream

Salt and freshly ground black pepper to taste

Put the fish pieces, with just enough fish stock to cover, into a large kettle. Bring the liquid to a boil and turn off the heat. When the fish is cooked through, remove the pieces to a bowl. Strain the stock several times through cheesecloth to remove all the impurities. Set aside.

Dice the salt pork and fry it gently in a large frying pan. When it has turned light brown, add the onions, shallots, garlic, celery, and paprika. Cook until the onions are translucent, then add 2 cups of the vermouth. Simmer until the liquid is reduced by half.

Pour this mixture into a large kettle and add 1½ quarts fish stock, making sure to use the reserved strained stock as well as the juices in the bowl. Add the tomato purée, lemon juice, thyme, and tarragon. Mix the cornstarch and the 6 tablespoons of vermouth and add half to three quarters of this mixture to the pot. Boil the liquid gently to thicken. If you prefer a thicker sauce for your stew, add the rest of the cornstarch-vermouth mixture.

Add the chopped parsley, the milk or cream, and the fish pieces and warm the stew over low heat. Stir gently, and taste for seasonings, adding salt and pepper as necessary. You may wish to add another cup of milk or cream. Everett Poole would not. Let the stew sit on a warm stove for at least half an hour to blend the flavors. Serve in large heated bowls.

Fish Stock

4 quarts water
2 carrots, washed but
  unscraped, cut in half
2 stalks celery, cut in half
8 pounds fish carcasses without
  gills

1 onion (peeled) studded with
  6 cloves
1 bay leaf
5 peppercorns

Put the water, carrots, celery, and fish carcasses into a large pot. Tie the clove-studded onion, bay leaf, and peppercorns in a cheesecloth bag and add it to the pot.

Bring the water to the "shiver," the stage just before simmer. Do not let it boil, because boiling disperses the sediment into the stock, spoiling its flavor and increasing its tendency to go sour.

Keep the stock at the shiver for an hour, periodically skimming off the sediment that rises to the top. Strain through cheesecloth. The stock will keep in the refrigerator for three or four days, or may be frozen.

Mussel Chowder

Serves 12 to 16

POOLE'S FISH MARKET, MENEMSHA, MASSACHUSETTS

A few years ago, the only way you could get mussels on Martha's Vineyard (or many other places) was to pick them off the rocks yourself, since the local fishermen didn't seem to think much of them. All that has changed, and though mussels may never replace the popular clam, more people are discovering that they are a marvelously delicate and versatile seafood.

This chowder is designed to be a first course. If you want to use it as a hearty main course, use 15 pounds of mussels and seven potatoes. The rest of the ingredients stay the same.

7 pounds mussels
1½ quarts water
1½-inch cube salt pork (or 4 tablespoons butter)
1 medium leek, diced
2 shallots, diced
1 medium onion, diced

½ cup dry white vermouth or wine
5 medium potatoes
6 tablespoons cornstarch
3 cups hot light cream or whole milk

Remove the seaweed "beards" from the mussels and scrub them clean. Check each mussel to be sure it contains meat, not mud, by rubbing the mussel between your fingers to see if it will open. This is important because one mudder can spoil the broth.

Steam the mussels in the water until they are just opened. Lift them out of the water immediately so that they don't overcook and become tough. Discard any that haven't opened (that means they were dead before steaming). Remove the meat from the shells and set aside.

Strain the broth through cheesecloth several times and set it aside.

Dice the salt pork and render the fat in a frying pan. Add the leek, shallots, and onion and sauté until tender. Add the vermouth or wine and simmer until the liquid is reduced by half.

Meanwhile, boil the potatoes, unskinned but cut in half, until just tender. Cool and then cut into ½-inch dice.

When the wine and onion mixture is reduced, transfer it to a large pot and add 2 quarts of the broth and the mussel meat. Mix the cornstarch with a small amount of the broth and add the mixture to the broth, stirring as you bring it to the simmer. (If you prefer a thicker chowder, make a paste of 2 more tablespoons of cornstarch and broth and stir it in.)

When the broth has reached the consistency you like, add the diced potatoes and the hot cream or milk — cream for a superb dish, milk for one that is almost as delicious but less fattening.

Seafood Gumbo *Serves 8 to 10*

THE AMERICAN CAFÉ MARKET, WASHINGTON, D.C.

If you can't find all the ingredients used in the original recipe, the suggested substitutes will still make an excellent gumbo. Chef Mark Caraluzzi emphasizes, however, that there is no substitute for the long, slow cooking of the roux, which gives the dish its rich color and flavor. The gumbo will keep for four or five days, but should not be frozen. When you reheat it, just get it hot — don't recook it.

8 tablespoons butter

9 tablespoons flour

1 large onion, sliced

1 green pepper, sliced

2 tablespoons finely chopped garlic

2 tablespoons chopped parsley

6 to 8 ripe tomatoes (or canned plum tomatoes)

4 Italian sausages, sliced ⅜ inch thick

½ pound Creole smoked sausage, sliced ⅜ inch thick (or kielbasa or any other smoked sausage)

1 quart plus 1 cup fish stock (or half bottled clam juice, half water)

¾ pound fresh okra (or 1 pound frozen okra), tips and stems removed, cut into 2-inch pieces

1 pound medium shrimp, peeled and deveined

2 bay leaves

1 teaspoon thyme

1 tablespoon salt

¾ teaspoon freshly ground black pepper

Pinch of cayenne

¾ pound crab claws with meat attached (or fillet of any firm, white fish, such as cod or halibut)

1 cup shucked oysters (approximately 12) with their juice

To make the roux: Use a Dutch oven or a pot with a heavy bottom to avoid scorching. Melt the butter and add the flour, stirring until all of the lumps are removed. Cook the roux over very low heat, stirring frequently, for about 25 minutes — until it is mahogany brown.

Add the onion, green pepper, garlic, and parsley, and cook for 10 minutes. Add the tomatoes, sausages, fish stock, okra, half the shrimp, and all the spices, and simmer for 1 hour.

Add the remaining shrimp, the crab claws, and the oysters. Bring the gumbo to a boil, reduce the heat to simmer, and cook for another 10 minutes. Let the dish stand for 10 to 15 minutes before serving. Serve with a side dish of rice.

Creole Fish Stew

THE FRUIT LADY, PHILADELPHIA

The fruit ladies (there are two of them) don't call their carry-out dishes "gourmet," but rather "just good food sensibly cooked." This is a good, filling dish for a crowd on a cold winter's night.

18 cloves garlic, minced
6 cups chopped onions
1 tablespoon chili pods
3 cups chopped green pepper
Sufficient olive oil for sautéing
1 cup Chablis
1 No.10 (105-ounce) can of tomatoes, or 6 pounds fresh tomatoes, diced

1 pint clam juice
2 bunches parsley, chopped
Salt and freshly ground black pepper to taste
2 pounds flounder fillets, cut into bite-sized chunks
2 pounds shrimp, shelled
1 pound crab meat
50 clams, steamed and shelled

Sauté the garlic, onions, chili pods, and green peppers in olive oil for 5 to 8 minutes. Add the Chablis and cook over medium heat 4 minutes more. Add the tomatoes, clam juice, parsley, salt, pepper, and fish and simmer for 15 minutes on low heat. Then add the shrimp, crab meat, and clams and simmer for 10 minutes more. Serve.

Shellfish Gazpacho

THE FISHMONGER, CAMBRIDGE

Like all the prepared dishes sold at The Fishmonger, this unusual variation on an old favorite is the creation of chef Thalia Large, who studied at the Rhode Island School of Design (which may account for the eye appeal of her dishes).

½ pound crab meat
½ pound medium or small shrimp, cooked, cooled, and peeled
1 medium cucumber
2 large ripe tomatoes
1 medium green pepper
1 medium red onion
3 tablespoons chopped parsley
2 quarts canned tomato juice, refrigerated

3 hard-boiled eggs
3 cloves garlic, minced
2 tablespoons Pommery mustard
¼ cup olive oil
1 tablespoon chili powder
Tabasco or hot sauce to taste
1 tablespoon Worcestershire sauce
½ cup lemon juice
1 teaspoon salt

Shred the crab meat and put it into a large bowl. Add the cooled shrimp. Peel the cucumber, scoop out the seeds, and cut it into a tiny dice. Add it to the bowl. Core, quarter, and seed the tomatoes. Chop into small pieces and add to the bowl. Chop the green pepper and the onion and add to the bowl along with the parsley. Pour in the tomato juice and refrigerate the soup base while you prepare the seasonings.

Separate the egg yolks from the whites. Save the whites and put the yolks into the container of a blender. Add the remaining ingredients and blend well. Stir the blended seasonings into the soup and taste. Make it spicier if you desire. Chop the egg whites and use them as a garnish. Serve very cold.

Chicken and Sausage Gumbo
Serves 6 to 8

CAMPBELL AND CO.'S "A MATTER OF TASTE,"
BOCA RATON, FLORIDA

Campbell's chef likes the combination of hot sausage and chicken in this flavorful gumbo.

1 pound chorizo (Spanish hot sausage), skinned and sliced into half-inch rounds
Vegetable oil (if needed)
3 whole chicken breasts cut into twelve pieces
4 teaspoons salt
Freshly ground black pepper
½ cup flour
Roux (see recipe below)
1 cup finely chopped onions

½ cup finely chopped scallions
1 cup finely chopped celery
1 cup finely chopped green peppers
3 quarts warm water
½ teaspoon Tabasco
1½ teaspoons cayenne
¼ cup finely chopped parsley
2 teaspoons gumbo filé
6 to 8 cups cooked long-grain rice

Fry the sausage rounds in a heavy skillet over low heat, turning them often until the bottom of the pan is filmed with fat. Increase the heat to moderate and continue to fry until sausage is browned. Drain on paper towels. There should be about ½ cup of fat in the skillet; if not, add some vegetable oil.

Pat the chicken dry and season with 2 teaspoons of salt and a few grindings of black pepper. Dredge the chicken pieces in flour, coating all sides and shaking off the excess. Brown the chicken pieces in the hot fat, turning frequently. As they brown, transfer to paper towels to drain.

Warm the roux over low heat in a cast-iron pot. When the roux is smooth and liquid, stir in the onions, scallions, and celery.

Cook over moderate heat, stirring frequently until the vegetables are soft. Add the green peppers. Then, stirring constantly, pour in the warm water in a slow, thin stream and bring to a boil over high heat. Add the sausage slices, chicken pieces, remaining salt, Tabasco, and cayenne. When the mixture returns to a boil, reduce the heat to low and partially cover the pot. Simmer for 2 hours. Remove the pot from the heat and skim the fat from the surface. Stir in the parsley and gumbo filé, and taste for seasonings. Ladle the gumbo into a heated turcen and serve at once, accompanied by the rice.

Roux

½ cup all-purpose flour   ½ cup vegetable oil

Combine the flour and oil in a heavy 10-inch skillct and stir to make a paste. Place over the lowest heat possible and simmer slowly for 45 minutes to 1 hour, stirring every 5 minutes until the roux is a rich dark brown. Makes about ¼ cup.

Cucumber Bisque

Serves 6

LE PETIT CHEF, MINNEAPOLIS

Few chefs have had as much impact on restaurant dining in the Twin Cities as Jean-Claude Tindillier, who arrived in Minnesota in the mid 1970s by way of Los Angeles, Venezuela, and Paris. As chef of Chouette, according to one restaurant critic, he produced a personal cuisine in the true spirit of French *haute cuisine*. Now, he's doing the same thing for *haute*-to-go.

Cold cucumber soup, which freezes very well, is a good thing to keep on hand in the summer. If you do freeze this one, complete it through the blending stage — and add the last four ingredients when you are ready to serve it. (Actually, you can freeze the entire recipe, but it will taste fresher this way.)

¾ cup chopped onion
1 tablespoon butter
1 tablespoon flour
3 large cucumbers, peeled and chopped
3½ cups chicken broth

1½ cups yogurt
2 small cucumbers, peeled and finely diced
¼ cup finely chopped parsley and chives, mixed
Salt and freshly ground black pepper to taste

Sauté the onions in the butter until they are translucent but not browned. Stir in the flour, the chopped large cucumbers, and the chicken broth. Bring to a boil and simmer, uncovered, for 45 minutes.

Pour the soup into a blender and blend until smooth. Chill. Stir in the yogurt, diced cucumbers, parsley, chives, salt, and pepper. Serve very cold.

Cold Asparagus Soup

BAGATELLE, BEVERLY HILLS

In 1971, André and Lucia Pister opened the first gourmet take-out operation in Los Angeles. André, a Burgundian who had been a chef for more than thirty years, announced firmly to his wife that whatever he could put on the table in his restaurant he wanted to make for home consumption, too. And that was how Bagatelle began. This soup is cool and refreshing on a hot summer's day.

1 onion, chopped
2 or 3 stalks celery, chopped
2 cloves garlic, minced
1 apple, chopped
Stems of 1 pound of asparagus (save the tips for garnish), chopped
Sufficient butter for sautéing
2 large potatoes, peeled and cubed

1 tablespoon curry powder
Chicken broth to cover
1½ cups half-and-half
Cayenne to taste
Dash of Worcestershire sauce
½ cup heavy cream, whipped
Sprinkling of grated coconut (optional)

Sauté the onion, celery, garlic, apple, and asparagus stems in a small amount of butter. Add the potatoes and the curry powder and cover with chicken broth. Cook, covered, over medium-low heat until the vegetables are tender. Remove the mixture from the heat and purée it in a food processor. Add the half-and-half, cayenne, and Worcestershire sauce. Chill well. Serve the soup garnished with the asparagus tips (which have been cooked until tender in hot, salted water) and whipped cream — and the grated coconut, if you wish.

Cold Raspberry Soup

Serves 6 to 8

REX'S MARKET DELICATESSEN, SEATTLE

If raspberries are in season, you can be sure that patrons of Rex's Market Delicatessen will find cold raspberry soup to take home for dinner. It is possible, though, to make this dish with frozen berries.

1 quart raspberries, fresh or frozen, unsweetened
Juice of one quarter of a lemon
2-inch cinnamon stick
3 cups water

⅓ cup sugar
¼ teaspoon salt
2 tablespoons cornstarch
¾ cup heavy cream

In a saucepan, combine the berries, lemon juice, cinnamon stick, water, sugar, and salt and bring to a boil. Simmer for 7 minutes. Make a paste of the cornstarch and a little water and add it to the soup. Stir and cook for 1 minute. Remove the cinnamon stick and force the remaining mixture through a sieve. Stir in the cream and chill well. Serve in chilled bowls.

Entrées

Swordfish Croquettes

Serves 4 to 6

NEUMAN & BOGDONOFF, NEW YORK CITY
   (UPPER EAST SIDE)

When the price of swordfish steaks is out of reach, Paul Neuman suggests buying the less expensive trimmings and turning them into swordfish croquettes.

3 eggs
¼ cup flat beer
About ¾ cup flour
1½ pounds swordfish trimmings, poached and ground
¼ pound onions, chopped

¼ pound green peppers, chopped
Garlic powder (optional)
Salt and freshly ground black pepper to taste
Vegetable oil for deep-frying

Beat the eggs and beer together. Add flour gradually, beating it in with a wire whisk, to the point where the batter drops off in clumps rather than ribbons when you raise the whisk. Set the batter aside for 1 hour.

Combine the ground swordfish, onions, peppers, and seasonings and add the batter. Stir to combine evenly.

Pour vegetable oil into a deep, heavy pot to a depth of about 4 inches. Heat the oil to 340°. To make the croquettes, fill a large spoon with the swordfish-batter mixture and use a smaller spoon to push balls about 1 to 2 inches in diameter into the hot fat, being careful not to drop the balls on top of each other. They will be cooked in 2 to 3 minutes, but you may need to do several batches. Drain well and serve with lemon wedges or tartar sauce.

Scallop and Shrimp Casserole

THE FISHMONGER, CAMBRIDGE

With her three children in school, Dorothy Borden decided to look for a job in her neighborhood. When she applied to The Fishmonger, a small shop she patronized, the owner asked her instead if she would like to buy the store. She took to the business like, er, a fish to water, and within two years had expanded into a larger area where all the cooking is done in the open for the customers to see. This casserole, which freezes well, is one of the shop's most popular, and most expensive, dishes.

1½ pounds medium shrimp
2 pounds sea scallops, or 2½ pounds tiny bay scallops
½ pound mushrooms
7 tablespoons butter
1 tablespoon olive oil
Salt and freshly ground black pepper to taste
1 large shallot, finely chopped

2 tablespoons flour
¼ teaspoon dry mustard
2 pinches cayenne
1¼ cups light cream
1 teaspoon brandy
1 teaspoon lemon juice
2 tablespoons chopped parsley
1 cup grated Gruyère cheese

Rinse, shell, and devein the shrimp. Pat dry and put them aside. Pull the "feet" (the tough muscle along the side) off the scallops. Rinse the scallops and pat dry. Cut large scallops, across the grain, into three or four slices. Cut medium-sized ones in half. Set the scallops aside. Clean the mushrooms and slice them thinly. Put a shallow, oven-proof dish into a 200° oven to warm.

Melt 2 tablespoons of the butter in a large, heavy skillet and sauté the mushrooms over medium-high heat until they are brown. Scrape them into a bowl and wash and dry the pan.

Put 2 tablespoons of the butter and the olive oil in the skillet and heat until bubbling. Lay the shrimp in the pan in one layer (if the pan is not large enough, do this in two steps), and sauté until the shrimp are red on the bottom. Flip them over, season with salt and pepper, reduce the heat, and cover the pan tightly. Cook them for about 2 minutes. They are done when the cut line down the back turns an opaque white. Using a slotted spoon, transfer the shrimp to a bowl. Leave the juices in the pan.

Add ½ cup of water to the pan juices, and deglaze. Separate the scallops with your fingers and put them in the pan in one layer. Poach them, covered, over low heat for 1½ to 2½ minutes, until they are just done. Remove them with a slotted spoon and add them to the bowl of mushrooms. Save the pan juices.

Toss the scallops and mushrooms together and check the seasonings. Spread them out in the warmed baking dish.

Split the shrimp in half lengthwise and place them, red side up, over the scallops and mushrooms. Cover the dish with a piece of buttered wax paper, and return it to the oven to keep warm while you prepare the sauce.

Melt the remaining 3 tablespoons of butter and sauté the shallots until they are soft. Add the flour, mustard, and cayenne, and cook for a few minutes over low heat, stirring constantly. Slowly add ½ cup of the reserved pan juices and the cream to the roux, beating them in with a whisk. Make sure to reach all sides and the bottom of the pan to prevent lumps. Cook, stirring constantly, until the sauce has thickened. Add the brandy and lemon juice and taste for seasonings. If you prefer a thinner sauce, add a little more cream. Stir in the parsley.

Pour the sauce over the shrimp and scallops. Turn the oven to broil.

Sprinkle the cheese over the top and brown the casserole in the broiler for a few minutes, watching it the whole time.

Note: The casserole may be prepared ahead of time. In that case, warm it up in the oven — but don't let it cook — before you sprinkle on the cheese and brown it.

Bay Scallops with Endive

Serves 8

DEMARCHELIER, NEW YORK CITY (UPPER EAST SIDE)

This elegant entrée is one of chef Marcello Iattoni's favorites. Born in Nantes, which he calls the Midwest of France, his background includes an apprenticeship at the Hôtel George V in Paris. If bay scallops are not available, cut sea scallops into quarters.

2 pounds endives
4 tablespoons butter
1 tablespoon sugar
Salt and freshly ground black
    pepper to taste

1 quart heavy cream
3 pounds bay scallops

Lay the endives sideways and cut them into ⅛-inch slices. Simmer them in the butter for 5 minutes over a low flame. Sprinkle with the sugar, salt, and pepper. Gradually add the cream, stirring constantly. Cook over a high flame until the sauce has been reduced by about two thirds. This should take about 20 minutes.

Rinse and pat dry the scallops and drop them into the cream sauce. Cook over low heat for about 5 minutes. Don't overcook, or the scallops will become rubbery. Correct the seasonings.

Serve with rice and a crisply cooked vegetable.

Bluefish and Mussels with Mustard Sauce

THE FISHMONGER, CAMBRIDGE   *Serves 4*

In addition to being an easy, inexpensive, and delicious dish, this is a perfect one to make when a fisherman friend presents you with more bluefish than you can eat in one sitting, since it freezes very well.

2 pounds mussels
1 bay leaf
Pinch of thyme
Handful of chopped parsley
   stems (if available)
Olive oil
Salt and freshly ground black
   pepper to taste
2 pounds bluefish, cut into four
   pieces

2 tablespoons butter
1 large shallot, finely chopped
1 tablespoon flour
1 cup light cream
4 teaspoons Pommery mustard
1 tablespoon finely chopped
   parsley

Wash the mussels and pull off the "beards." Put the bay leaf, thyme, and parsley stems into a big pot with a lid. Put about ½ inch of water in the pot and bring it to a boil with the lid on.

When the water is boiling hard, throw the mussels in quickly and put the lid back on. Steam the mussels for about 5 minutes, until the shells open. Drain the mussels, discarding any that have not opened. Strain the broth and set it aside. Shell the mussels and set aside.

Preheat the oven to 350°. Grease a baking dish with olive oil. Sprinkle it with salt and pepper. Place the pieces of bluefish, spaced slightly apart, on the dish. Brush them with a little oil and season with salt and pepper. Cover the dish tightly with foil and place in the oven. Thick bluefish takes 20 to 25 minutes to bake, thin fish

72

about 15 minutes. Check occasionally for doneness. The fish is cooked when it flakes when pierced with a fork.

While the fish is cooking, prepare the sauce. Melt the butter and sauté the shallots until they are soft. Stir in the flour and cook the roux over medium heat for a few minutes. Whisk in ½ cup of the reserved mussel broth and the cream in a steady stream. Whisk over medium heat, making sure to get rid of all lumps, until the sauce is thickened. Stir in the mustard and check for seasonings. Fold in the mussels and the chopped parsley.

Place the bluefish on a warmed platter and top with the sauce.

Shrimp Ouisie   *Serves 4*

OUISIE'S TABLE AND THE TRAVELING
BROWN BAG LUNCH CO., HOUSTON

The brown bags started traveling fourteen years ago: Every weekday morning Elouise Cooper packed a giant picnic hamper, which her husband took to his office, where twelve regular customers paid $1.50 for her three-course lunch. The real business (which now has a staff of forty and serves 550 customers a day) opened seven years ago near Rice University and the Texas Medical Center. Last spring, Ouisie had a birthday party; turning the tables a bit, she invited her regular customers to bring a covered dish to a potluck supper. They say some of the best cooks in Houston showed up. Ouisie serves this dish in individual 8-ounce ramekins.

Olive oil

½ pound fresh spinach, washed and stemmed

Freshly grated nutmeg

¾ cup heavy cream, lightly whipped

24 large raw Gulf shrimp, peeled

4 strips crisply cooked bacon

Fresh tomato sauce (see recipe below)

Grated Parmesan cheese

Drizzle a little olive oil into each ramekin. Make a layer of spinach at the bottom and dust it lightly with nutmeg. Don't go overboard on the nutmeg. Spoon the heavy cream over the spinach and nestle six shrimp in one layer in each ramekin. Crumble the bacon over the shrimp and spoon the tomato sauce over all. Bake in a preheated 450° oven for a few minutes, until bubbly. Before the last few minutes of cooking, sprinkle a little Parmesan cheese over each ramekin. Serve with French bread to dip in the juices.

This dish is also excellent when oysters are substituted for the shrimp. It makes a juicier dish and the bread is a must.

Fresh Tomato Sauce

Light olive oil

½ bunch finely chopped green onions

2 large garlic cloves, minced

4 ripe tomatoes, peeled, seeded, and coarsely chopped

¾ cup dry white vermouth

Salt to taste

Fresh basil, if available

In a little olive oil, sauté the green onions until they are just soft. Stir in the garlic, and a little more olive oil if needed. Add the tomatoes. Simmer a few minutes and add the vermouth. Stir from the bottom, cover, and simmer for 5 minutes. Taste for salt. Add chopped fresh basil to taste, if available.

Salmon Steaks with Golden Caviar and Parsley Sauce

Serves 4

THE WATERGATE CHEFS, WASHINGTON, D.C.

American Golden Caviar, a special brand of Great Lakes whitefish roe, is sold frozen in plastic jars in specialty food shops like The Watergate Chefs. It is much less expensive than Russian caviar, much less salty than the ordinary whitefish roe, and the eggs are tinier and prettier than those of salmon caviar — all in all, it's worth seeking out. Chef Jean-Louis Palladin is the Watergate chef who created this beautiful dish.

2 bunches parsley
4 shallots
6 tablespoons dry white vermouth
Pinch of thyme
1 quart fish stock
2 cups cream

Salt and freshly ground black pepper to taste
4 salmon steaks, each weighing about 8 ounces
Olive oil
8 ounces Golden Caviar

Remove the stems from the parsley and poach the leaves briefly in highly salted water. Drain the parsley and mince in a food processor.

Chop the shallots finely. Heat the vermouth, add the shallots and the thyme, and reduce the liquid by half. Add the fish stock and reduce by half. Add the cream and reduce again by half. At this point, the sauce should be of a creamy consistency. Season with salt and pepper.

Sauté the salmon steaks lightly in olive oil, about 2 minutes on each side, until done.

Whisk the puréed parsley into the sauce. Reheat the sauce, but do not let it boil. Stir in the caviar.

Place one salmon steak in the center of each plate and surround it with the sauce. Serve immediately.

75

Sautéed Shrimp with Zucchini   *Serves 6*

SI BON, SANIBEL, FLORIDA

This shrimp and zucchini dish can easily be made and re-frigerated well in advance of the guests' arrival time. When reheating it, do so briefly in a high-temperature oven. Over-cooking will make the shrimp tough.

1¼ pounds small zucchini
6 stalks celery
1⅔ pounds shrimp (allow 6 or 7 per person if they are 21 to 25 to the pound)
3 tablespoons olive oil
2 tomatoes, peeled, seeded, and chopped

2 tablespoons chopped parsley
3 cloves garlic, finely chopped
1 teaspoon thyme·
3 tablespoons butter
Salt and freshly ground black pepper to taste

Scrub the zucchini and cut them into diagonal slices about the same thickness as the shrimp. String the celery (if necessary) and cut it on the diagonal into ½-inch-thick pieces. Peel the shrimp.

Heat half the olive oil in a large pot. Sauté the zucchini for 5 minutes over medium-high heat and set it aside. Sauté the celery for 5 minutes and set it aside. Add the remaining oil and sauté the shrimp over high heat for 2 minutes. Off the heat, combine the zucchini, celery, and shrimp. Add the remaining ingredients and stir to combine.

Refrigerate the dish until you are ready to use it. Serve it, once reheated, with white rice.

Cold Curried Fish

Serves 6 to 8

FÊTE ACCOMPLIE, WASHINGTON, D.C.

This dish had its origins among the Cape Malays, who settled on the southernmost point of Africa. It can be served either as a first course or as a main dish with potatoes and salad. It is a favorite creation of Jake Martin, who is co-owner of this shop with Millie White.

2 pounds 1-inch-thick fish
   steaks (cod, haddock, or
   turbot)
½ cup vegetable oil
2 large onions, sliced into
   ⅛-inch rounds
½ cup brown sugar
3 green chili peppers, seeded
   and chopped

1 tablespoon chopped ginger
2 bay leaves, crumbled
Salt to taste
2 tablespoons curry powder,
   preferably Madras
1 cup cider vinegar
1 cup water

Pat the fish dry with paper towels and sauté it in ¼ cup of the oil for 2 to 3 minutes on each side. Drain the fish on paper towels.

Cook the onions in the remaining ¼ cup of oil for 5 minutes and set aside. Combine the sugar, chilis, ginger, bay leaves, salt, and curry powder in a saucepan and stir over low heat for 2 minutes. Add the vinegar and water and simmer this marinade, uncovered, for 10 minutes. Cool.

Cut the fish into 2-inch squares and lay about a third of it in the bottom of a glass or enamel dish. Place a third of the onion mixture over it, then a third of the marinade. Add another layer of fish and top it again with onions and marinade. Repeat for a third time. Cover the dish tightly with plastic wrap and refrigerate it for at least two days and as many as seven before serving.

Chicken, Shrimp, and Scallop Provençal

NEUMAN & BOGDONOFF, NEW YORK CITY   *Serves 6*
    (UPPER EAST SIDE)

New York's Upper East Side is a mecca for patrons of gourmet carry-out food shops. Although this is a relatively new one, its owners, Stacy Bogdonoff and Paul Neuman, were both associated with Neuman's family's Lexington Avenue Rosedale Fish Market. This marvelously hearty company dish is especially convenient because you can prepare it ahead of time and put it together at the last minute.

About ½ cup olive oil
18 raw shrimp, peeled and deveined
18 sea or bay scallops
6 skinless boned chicken breasts (12 halves)
2 pounds onions, sliced
½ pound green pepper, sliced lengthwise
½ pound red pepper, sliced lengthwise

1 19-ounce can Italian plum tomatoes, drained and seeded
3 generous tablespoons tomato paste
6 medium (8 small) cloves garlic, finely chopped
Pinch of ground saffron
Pinch of basil
Pinch of oregano
Salt and freshly ground black pepper to taste

In a good, fruity olive oil, over moderate to high heat, sauté the shrimp until just pink and the scallops until just firm. Remove them with a slotted spoon and set aside. Add the chicken to the pan and sauté until just cooked. Remove and set aside.

    In the same pan, adding more olive oil if needed, sauté the onions and peppers until soft but not brown. Add the remaining ingredients as well as the juices from the sautéed shrimp, scallops, and chicken. (If necessary, a little chicken broth may be added to the sauce if there is not enough liquid.)

Bring the mixture to the boil and simmer it over low heat while you prepare the chicken. Cut the chicken breasts into long finger-shaped pieces, about five or six to each breast half. Add them to the simmering sauce. Add the seafood just before serving.

Serve with rice or pasta or toasted garlic bread.

Pollo al Limone (Lemon Chicken)   *Serves 4*
VIVANDE, SAN FRANCISCO

This creation of Vivande's proprietor-chef Carlo Middione is particularly popular with the diet-conscious, for it requires neither salt nor additional fat in the cooking.

A 2¾-pound roasting chicken
1 large lemon

Freshly ground black pepper to taste

Preheat the oven to 375°.

With a double-tined cooking fork or a trussing needle, pierce the lemon almost clear through everywhere you can, twenty to thirty times. Set aside any juice that leaks out.

Remove the small pads of fat from the vent of the chicken and discard them (unless you are going to use them in other cooking). Place the lemon and any of the extra juice in the cavity of the bird and truss the bird with string or metal skewers. Season the chicken with pepper.

Place the chicken in a small roasting pan and roast for 1 hour and 10 minutes. When the bird is done, let it rest outside the oven for 10 or 15 minutes, covered with oiled or buttered parchment paper. This will make it juicier. Serve.

Breast of Chicken with Prosciutto and Sage

WASHINGTON MARKET, NEW YORK CITY (TRIBECA)   *Serves 6*

This handsome shop in an old market building is located in Tribeca (*Tri*angle *Be*low *Ca*nal Street), the area which is to Manhattan in the 1980s what SoHo (*So*uth of *Ho*uston Street) was in the 1970s — a mecca for artists and other loft-dwellers. The market sells virtually every kind of food, as well as prepared dishes to take out. This is an elegant one, not at all hard to make.

3 whole chicken breasts
Flour
5 tablespoons unsalted butter
1 teaspoon dried sage
6 slices prosciutto

⅔ cup chicken stock or canned chicken broth
½ cup dry white vermouth
Salt and freshly ground black pepper to taste

Remove the skin from the chicken breasts, and bone them. Flatten each half between two pieces of wax paper. Lightly dust with flour.

Melt 4 tablespoons of butter in a skillet and sauté the breasts on one side without browning. Turn the breasts over and sauté the other side. Sprinkle the breasts with sage and lay a slice of prosciutto over each one. Quickly add the stock and vermouth to the pan and simmer for 3 to 5 minutes, spooning the liquid over the chicken as it cooks. Remove the breasts to a heated platter.

Reduce the sauce in the pan until it reaches a glazelike consistency. Off the heat, stir in the remaining tablespoon of butter. Pour the sauce over the chicken and serve.

Stuffed Chicken Breasts with Lemon Caper Sauce

Serves 4

POULET, BERKELEY

She was a Boston social worker and he was a research biologist when they met at a potluck supper. Out of their mutual interest in fine food, Marilyn Rinzler and Bruce Aidells decided they could offer a gourmet alternative to the fast-food establishments. The result was Poulet, an unusual carry-out shop that specializes in chicken and duck dishes of every kind. Of the two hundred fifty different poultry dishes chef Aidells has served up, this is one of the most popular.

1 pound spinach, washed and stemmed
1 sweet Italian sausage with fennel
1 cup finely chopped leeks
2 shallots, finely chopped
½ pound cooked ham, finely chopped
½ cup bread crumbs
¼ cup Parmesan cheese
¼ teaspoon tarragon
1 tablespoon chopped parsley

1 "large" egg, lightly beaten
Salt and freshly ground black pepper to taste
2 whole chicken breasts (1 pound each)
Flour for dredging
¼ cup butter
¼ cup olive oil
¼ cup dry white wine
2 cloves garlic, minced
Juice of 1 or 2 lemons
1 tablespoon capers
1 tablespoon chopped parsley

Blanch the spinach. Drain, chop, and set it aside.

Squeeze the sausage meat out of the casing and fry it. Add to the fat and sausage the leeks, shallots, and ham, and cook over low heat until the vegetables are limp and transparent. Transfer the mixture to a bowl and add the spinach, bread crumbs, Parmesan cheese, tarragon, parsley, and egg. Stir well, and season with salt and pepper.

Bone the chicken breasts. Cut a pocket in each half. Stuff with the stuffing mixture.

Season the chicken breasts with salt and pepper. Dredge them in flour and fry in the oil and butter until golden on each side.

Transfer the breasts to a platter. Deglaze the pan with the wine. Add the garlic and cook down until the wine becomes syrupy. Add the lemon juice, capers, and parsley. Pour over the chicken and serve immediately.

Sautéed Breast of Chicken Smitane — *Serves 4*
CAVIAR ETCETERA, WOODBURY, LONG ISLAND

In the days when Long Island's North Shore was known as the Gold Coast, many mansions of this area had their own chefs. Today few of those mansions are still in private hands, and the chefs who cater North Shore parties are likely to be in the employ of a gourmet food shop like Caviar Etcetera.

Since it takes twelve hours of cooking to make a rich stock for a *demi-glace,* you may substitute canned brown or Espagnole sauce for the *demi-glace* in this chicken dish.

4 tablespoons flour
Salt and freshly ground black
   pepper to taste
4 whole chicken breasts,
   skinned and boned
4 tablespoons butter
4 tablespoons olive oil

8 tablespoons chopped shallots
2 cups *smitane* (sour cream
   and sweet heavy cream
   mixed half and half)
1 cup *demi-glace*
4 tablespoons chopped parsley

Lightly flour and salt and pepper the chicken breasts and sauté them in the butter and olive oil until they are golden brown. Remove them from the pan and drain.

In the same pan, sauté the shallots sprinkled with the flour left over from dredging the chicken (to absorb the fat). Add the *smitane* and cook for 5 minutes over medium heat. Return the chicken to the skillet. Add the *demi-glace* and cook the chicken over low heat for 12 minutes. Correct the seasonings. Add the parsley. Serve on a bed of sorrel or fresh spinach that has been blanched and lightly sautéed in butter. (If spinach is used, it should be flavored with a pinch of nutmeg.)

Poulet Dijonnaise   *Serves 6 to 8*

COMPLETE CUISINE LTD., ANN ARBOR

This is one of the most-asked-for recipes from Complete Cuisine, the Ann Arbor cooking school, restaurant, and gourmet food shop.

4 large whole chicken breasts, skinned and boned

Salt and freshly ground black pepper to taste

4 to 5 tablespoons unsalted butter

½ cup imported Dijon mustard

2 cups *crème fraîche* or heavy cream

Cut the chicken into 1-inch-wide strips and sprinkle the strips with salt and pepper. Sauté them in butter over medium heat for about 4 minutes, until they are golden brown. Transfer the chicken to an oven-proof platter and keep warm.

Stir the mustard into the remaining butter and juices in the pan, scraping up the bits. Beat in the *crème fraîche* with a whisk.

Reduce the heat to low and cook the sauce until it has reduced by one fourth. It should be thick and velvety. Adjust the seasonings and strain the sauce over the chicken pieces. Serve with green fettuccine and a salad.

Breast of Chicken Marsala — *Serves 6 to 8*
LES CHEFETTES, GREAT NECK, LONG ISLAND

Rhoda Kafer and Sue Steger used to be cooking teachers, but they found they enjoyed cooking even more than they did teaching. So, more than a dozen years ago, they began Les Chefettes. They and their staff prepare entrées, desserts, hors d'oeuvres, quiches, and all sorts of tea breads — as well as a complete line of foods for special diets and dieters — for enthusiastic customers. This is one of their entrées that can easily be frozen and reheated.

4 whole chicken breasts, skinned and boned
1 cup plus 2 tablespoons flour
2 lightly beaten eggs
2 cups unseasoned bread crumbs
1 tablespoon butter
2 tablespoons light vegetable oil

½ pound fresh mushrooms, sliced
⅓ cup dry Marsala
1 clove garlic, pressed
1 cup chicken broth
A few slices fresh lemon
Salt and pepper to taste

Dredge the chicken breasts in 1 cup of the flour and shake off the excess thoroughly; dip them in the beaten eggs and then in the bread crumbs. Melt the butter and oil in a large skillet; when it is hot and bubbly, add the chicken and sauté it until golden brown on both sides. Remove the chicken from the pan. Add the mushrooms to the pan and cook them over a medium flame for about 1 minute. Sprinkle the remaining 2 tablespoons of flour over them and cook them for an additional 30 seconds, making sure that they do not burn. Add the Marsala, garlic, chicken broth, and lemon slices. Stir the sauce until slightly thickened. Return the chicken to the sauce, season with salt and pepper, cover, and cook over medium heat for 10 to 15 minutes.

Saucy Stuffed Chicken   *Serves 6*
GOODIES TO GO, LEXINGTON, MASSACHUSETTS

For many years, Gaye Pickrel was the owner of a restaurant called The Bellybutton in Greenwich Village. This chicken recipe was devised to please her patrons there. She suggests serving it with rice pilaf.

3 whole chicken breasts, boned and skinned
2 pounds fresh spinach, washed and stemmed, or 1 10-ounce package frozen spinach
1 large onion
8 tablespoons butter
Salt and freshly ground black pepper to taste
6 slices cooked ham

6 slices Swiss cheese
½ cup chicken broth
½ cup dry white wine
1½ tablespoons flour
Juice of 2 lemons
1 cup heavy cream
1 pound mushrooms, sliced
A few sprigs of parsley (for garnish)

Split the chicken breasts in two and pound them between two pieces of wax paper with a mallet or rolling pin. Blanch the fresh spinach or cook the frozen spinach and drain it thoroughly. Dice the onion and sauté it with 3 tablespoons of the butter. Add the drained spinach to the onions and stir in the salt and pepper. Let the mixture cool.

Place a slice of ham and a slice of cheese on top of each pounded chicken breast. Top with a mound of the spinach filling. Carefully roll the chicken breasts and place them in a baking dish, seam side down. When all the breasts are filled and rolled, pour the chicken broth and ¼ cup of the white wine over them. Place the chicken in a preheated 350° oven for 20 to 25 minutes. Remove it from the oven and carefully strain off the liquid. Set the liquid aside, and keep the chicken breasts warm while you make the sauce.

Make a roux with the remaining butter and the flour and gradually add the reserved liquid, the rest of the wine, the lemon juice, and the cream, stirring until the sauce thickens. Add the sliced mushrooms and continue simmering the sauce until the mushrooms are soft. Pour the sauce over the chicken breasts. Garnish with fresh parsley and serve.

Chicken Escabeche *Serves 4*

DEAN & DeLUCA, NEW YORK CITY (SoHo)

A favorite ingredient of chef Felipe Rojas-Lombardi's cuisine is achiote oil, which he uses like paprika to flavor and color a variety of foods, such as meats, poultry, fish, and savory pastries. The annatto seeds, which are the main ingredient, are available at gourmet food shops. Although only 2 tablespoons of the achiote oil is used in this cold chicken dish, it's worth making because the oil keeps for a year in the refrigerator.

A 3½-pound chicken, cut into
serving pieces

Oil for deep-frying

2 tablespoons achiote oil (see
recipe below)

3 tablespoons olive or
vegetable oil

1 pound pearl onions, peeled

1 carrot, peeled and cut into
thick julienne

1 whole hot green pepper

6 to 8 black peppercorns

1 bay leaf

2 cloves garlic

4 cups red wine vinegar

1 cup dry white wine

1 sweet green pepper, cut in
½-inch strips

1 sweet red pepper, cut in
½-inch strips

4 lettuce leaves

Feta cheese and black olives
(for garnish)

Deep-fry the chicken until the pieces are crisp and golden. Set them
on a towel to drain.

In a large skillet, heat the achiote oil and the olive or vegetable
oil. As soon as it is hot, add the onions and sauté them quickly for 3
to 5 minutes. stirring constantly. Add the carrots, hot green pepper,
peppercorns, bay leaf, garlic, wine vinegar, and white wine. Bring to
a boil and remove from heat. Add the chicken and the sweet peppers and refrigerate overnight, being sure that the ingredients are
covered by the marinade. Serve the chicken on a lettuce leaf. Garnish with feta cheese and black olives. Refrigerated, this dish will
keep for a week. Or you can freeze it indefinitely.

Achiote Oil

½ cup annatto seeds

1 cup vegetable oil

1 or 2 fresh or dried chili
peppers

Place the annatto seeds, oil, and chili pepper in a saucepan over low
heat. Slowly bring the mixture to the boiling point. Remove it from
the heat and let it cool to room temperature. Strain through several
layers of cheesecloth. Refrigerate.

Chicken Indienne

Serves 4 to 6

FORMAGGIO KITCHEN, CAMBRIDGE

When Norma Wasserman was living in London, studying painting, she became enchanted with the daily experience of shopping for food in Soho, where she got to know the fishmonger, the greengrocer, the butcher, and the baker. Three years ago, following the success of her cheese and sandwich shop in Harvard Square, she opened Formaggio Kitchen, with the idea of re-creating that European shopping experience. Today, with two other specialty food shops next door, a hitherto nondescript block on Huron Avenue has been transformed into a lively gourmet shopping center.

This recipe is an adaptation of one Norma found in an old Chinese cookbook in London. It won a "Best of Boston" award from *Boston* magazine in 1981.

½ cup flour
4 tablespoons curry powder
4 tablespoons cumin
2 tablespoons turmeric
1 tablespoon cayenne or to taste
1 tablespoon paprika
1 pound boned chicken breasts, cut in bite-size pieces

1 tablespoon oil
1 tablespoon butter
4 onions, diced
2 or 3 cloves garlic, crushed
4 tomatoes, diced
½ cup raisins
½ cup chutney
Salt and freshly ground black pepper to taste

Mix together the flour, curry, cumin, turmeric, and cayenne. Dredge the chicken pieces in this curry mixture until they are thoroughly coated.

Heat oil in a sauté pan and sear the chicken pieces quickly until they are just firm. Set aside. Add a bit more oil to the pan and add the onions and garlic. Cover the pan and cook for a few minutes until the onions release their juices and soften. Add the tomatoes, raisins, and chutney, and simmer, covered, for 5 to 10 minutes, or until a sauce has formed. (Add a small amount of chicken broth if the sauce seems too thick.) Add the chicken and simmer for 10 minutes. Season with salt and pepper. Serve hot over boiled rice.

Note: This is also very good served at room temperature as a curried chicken salad.

Quick Chicken Curry   Serves 6
PROOF OF THE PUDDING, ATLANTA

It was the large community of busy young professional people in Atlanta these days that led North Carolinian Kay Goldstein to switch from a catering business to a gourmet take-out shop. One ever-popular entrée has been this crispy, crunchy stir-fried chicken curry. The sauce also makes a fine dip for raw vegetables or cold steamed artichokes.

Curry Sauce

1 cup sour cream
½ cup mayonnaise
Juice of 1 lemon
1 minced green onion
2 tablespoons minced parsley

2 tablespoons medium-hot curry powder
½ teaspoon Dijon mustard
½ teaspoon paprika
Salt, freshly ground black pepper, and Tabasco to taste

Mix all the ingredients together. Let the sauce stand, refrigerated, for a while so all of the flavors are melded. This recipe makes 1½ cups of sauce; you will have half left over for another time.

Curried Chicken

2½ pounds boned, skinned
  chicken breasts, cubed

1½ tablespoons peanut oil

2 green peppers cut into
  1-inch dice

1 medium red onion, cut into
  1-inch dice

2 ounces almonds

2 ounces raisins

¾ cup curry sauce (see recipe
  on previous page)

¾ cup plain yogurt

1 cup chicken stock

1 tablespoon medium-hot
  curry powder or
  ½ tablespoon mild and
  ½ tablespoon hot

Salt and freshly ground black
  pepper to taste

Sauté the chicken briefly in the peanut oil. Add the peppers and onions and quickly sauté them, being sure that they remain crisp and bright. Add the remaining ingredients, bring to a simmer, and turn off the heat. This curry reheats nicely.

Caviar-Style Duckling
Serves 4

CAVIAR ETCETERA, WOODBURY, LONG ISLAND

Although there's no caviar in this recipe — it's named in honor of the shop that sells it — it *is* a grand dish.

A 4½-pound duckling

¼ cup apricot brandy

Stuffing

½ cup blanched wild rice

¼ cup long-grain rice

½ cup golden raisins

½ cup pitted prunes, cut in
  quarters

½ cup pitted dates, cut in
  quarters

½ cup blanched or canned
  chestnuts

½ cup brown sugar

¼ cup honey

Glaze

2 tablespoons apricot glaze
(available in many
supermarkets)
2 tablespoons honey

2 tablespoons orange
marmalade
2 tablespoons brandy
2 tablespoons brown sugar

Rub the inside of the duckling with the apricot brandy. Set aside.

Mix the stuffing ingredients together and stuff the duck. Place the duck on a wire rack in an open roasting pan and roast it for 1 hour in a preheated 300° oven.

Mix the glaze ingredients and apply them to the duck. Continue to roast the duck, brushing it with glaze every 30 minutes until it is done — about 2½ hours total cooking time.

THE FISHMONGER

Chicken Kuwayaki   *Serves 3*

A MOVEABLE FEAST, PHILADELPHIA

From an old pharmacy, fitted out with its original apothecary cases as well as modern glass freezer cabinets, Ruth Mellman, Betty Moloznik, and Georgia Parks supply the academic community of Philadelphia with sustenance for box-lunch seminars, faculty teas, cocktail parties, and theater openings at the Annenberg Center.

The only exotic ingredient called for in this dish is *mirin,* a sweet rice cooking wine, available in Oriental food markets.

½ cup flour
1 pound boned chicken breasts, cut into bite-size pieces
6 tablespoons salad oil

6 tablespoons water
9 tablespoons *mirin*
4½ tablespoons soy sauce
4 teaspoons sugar
1 bunch scallions, chopped

Sprinkle flour generously over the chicken. Add the salad oil to a heated wok, heat the oil, and quickly brown the chicken.

Mix the water, *mirin*, soy sauce, and sugar in a saucepan and simmer for 3 minutes.

Pour this sauce into the wok, coating the chicken well. Cook over medium heat until the sauce thickens. Stir in the scallions and cook for 2 minutes. Serve with rice.

Swedish Potted Beef with Lingonberries and Horseradish
Serves 8 to 10

THE CHARCUTERIE, WELLESLEY, MASSACHUSETTS

After you've majored in philosophy or English, what do you do next? These days, it seems, you are likely to get a job in a gourmet food shop, study cooking, and then go into business for yourself. Which is just what two friends, John Gordon (English) and Michael Staub (philosophy and classics) did when they graduated from Tufts.

One of the added virtues of this excellent potted beef is that it freezes very well.

3 tablespoons vegetable oil
An 8-pound rolled chuck roast
8-ounce jar imported
  lingonberries
½ cup plus 3 tablespoons
  freshly grated horseradish
3 cups veal stock (or College
  Inn beef broth)

Salt and freshly ground black
  pepper to taste
12 to 15 new potatoes
8 carrots, each cut into four
  pieces
1 cup heavy cream
Juice of half a lemon

In a sauté pan, heat the oil until it smokes. Brown the roast on all sides. Set it aside and preheat the oven to 325°.

Put the lingonberries, ½ cup of the horseradish, the veal stock, and salt and pepper in a saucepan and simmer for 5 minutes.

Place the roast in an oven-proof braising pan, just large enough to hold it comfortably. Pour the simmering liquid over the roast; it should come about two thirds of the way up the side of the beef. Cover the meat with foil and put the lid on the pan. Place the pan in the oven and cook for 2 to 2½ hours.

When the meat is almost done, boil the carrots and potatoes in a large amount of water until they are just tender. Set them aside.

Remove the meat from the pan and skim off the fat from the cooking liquid. Put the fat-free braising liquid in a saucepan and reduce it over medium heat by one third. Add the heavy cream and reduce by one third. Add the remaining horseradish and the lemon juice. Season with salt and pepper. Taste, and adjust the seasonings if necessary.

Slice the meat and arrange the vegetables around it. Pour the sauce over all.

The dish may be prepared in advance and reheated for 20 minutes in a 300° oven. Or it may be frozen and reheated (unthawed) for an hour in a 325° oven.

Stuffed Flank Steak
Serves 4 to 6

DEAN & DeLUCA, NEW YORK CITY (SoHo)

Now New Yorkers can go off to their summer homes on the eastern end of Long Island secure in the knowledge that they won't have to survive on hot dogs and hamburgers — Dean & DeLuca has a shop in East Hampton. Thank heavens!

You can serve this flank steak hot, but it makes a wonderful cold buffet dish garnished with cornichons or Italian sun-dried tomatoes (*pumate*). It refrigerates well for up to a week.

1 pound lean ground pork
2 pounds chopped mushrooms (squeezed dry in the corner of a towel)
1 small onion, finely chopped
1 teaspoon tarragon
⅛ teaspoon mace
Salt and freshly ground black pepper to taste

A 1½-to-2-pound flank steak, with a pocket cut in it
1 clove garlic
1 teaspoon salt
⅛ teaspoon cumin seed
1 tablespoon dark soy sauce
1 teaspoon vinegar, preferably balsamic vinegar
⅛ teaspoon sesame oil

In a mixing bowl, combine the pork, mushrooms, onion, tarragon, mace, salt, and pepper. Mix thoroughly. Fill the pocket in the flank steak with this stuffing and sew it closed tightly. Set aside.

Use a mortar and pestle to pulverize the garlic, salt, and cumin seed. Add the soy sauce, vinegar, and sesame oil, and mix. Rub both sides of the flank steak with this mixture and let it sit for 1 hour in a cool place.

Preheat the oven to 400°. Place the stuffed flank steak on a rack and roast it for 30 minutes. Turn it over and roast for another 30 minutes. Remove it from the oven and let it sit for 10 minutes before serving, if you plan to eat it right away. If it is to be served cold, let it cool before refrigerating.

Easy Beef Stew

FÊTE ACCOMPLIE, WASHINGTON, D.C.

One of the newest of Washington's carry-out shops, this was also the only one to receive a four-star rating from the food editor of the *Washington Post.* The shop is owned by two women, Millie White and Jake Martin, who met when they were both looking at the same empty shop, which was too big for either of them to handle alone. The real-estate agent suggested they join forces — and Fête Accomplie was a fait accompli.

This beef stew is proof that delicious food doesn't have to be complicated to make.

3 pounds chuck, cut in 1½-inch cubes

1 large onion, diced

12 baby carrots

1 sweet red pepper cut in ½-inch strips

1 pound small fresh mushrooms, cleaned

2 small turnips, cut in chunks

4 fresh tomatoes, cut in wedges

½ cup bread crumbs

2 tablespoons instant tapioca

2 cups red wine

Salt and freshly ground black pepper to taste

½ pound small frozen pearl onions, thawed

Put all the ingredients except the pearl onions in a Dutch oven with a tight-fitting lid. Bake in a preheated 325° oven for 4 hours. Don't peek! Add the onions after the stew is removed from the oven. Serve with a crusty bread and green salad.

Hungarian Beef Goulash

Serves 4 to 6

KENESSEY GOURMETS INTERNATIONALE, CHICAGO

This goulash is given a special touch by the addition of a cup of Burgundy to the gravy.

2½ pounds lean stew beef, cubed
½ cup vegetable oil
1 large Spanish onion, chopped
1 tablespoon Hungarian paprika
1 cup cold water
1 small tomato, chopped

1 green pepper, chopped
2 cups quartered mushrooms
1 cup Burgundy
Salt to taste
½ teaspoon freshly ground black pepper
1 cup sour cream

Brown the meat in the oil in a Dutch oven and remove the meat with a slotted spoon. Sauté the onion in the oil remaining in the pan. Add the paprika and the cold water immediately to prevent scorching. Return the meat to the Dutch oven. Add the tomato and half of the green pepper and simmer the meat, covered, for 1½ hours. Twenty minutes before you are ready to remove it, add the mushrooms, Burgundy, and the remaining green pepper. Season with the salt and pepper. Add the sour cream just before serving, or pass it in a separate dish. Serve with noodles or boiled potatoes.

Pasticcio

Serves 8 to 10

BALDUCCI'S, NEW YORK CITY (GREENWICH VILLAGE)

Although it's indoors in New York City, Balducci's reminds one of the experience of shopping in a colorful, bustling, European market square. Among the 120 employees who keep everything moving here are Marie and Louis Balducci's children, nieces, nephews, and grandchildren. This dish happens to be an ideal one to serve when children are on the guest list.

1 small onion, finely chopped
2 tablespoons olive oil
1 pound ground beef
1 pound ricotta cheese
8 ounces mozzarella cheese, coarsely grated
2 eggs, lightly beaten

⅓ cup grated Parmesan cheese
1 cup cooked peas
2 cups your favorite tomato sauce
½ pound egg fettuccine
½ pound spinach fettuccine
Freshly ground black pepper to taste

Sauté the chopped onion in the olive oil until it is transparent. Add the ground beef and sauté until it loses its red color. Set aside.

In a large bowl, combine the ricotta, mozzarella, eggs, Parmesan cheese, peas, and 1 cup of the tomato sauce. Mix well and set aside.

Cook the fettuccine in plenty of salted boiling water. Fresh pasta will be ready in a matter of seconds, dry in 2 to 3 minutes. It should be cooked only partially and be still brittle when drained. After it is drained, add it to the cheese mixture. Add the meat and mix well. Add pepper to taste.

Pour the mixture into a buttered baking dish. Pour the remaining tomato sauce over the top. Bake in a preheated 300° oven for 30 minutes. Remove it from the oven, and let the *pasticcio* set before serving.

Beef in Burgundy
Serves 10 to 12

THE CHAPLAIN'S PANTRY, TACOMA, WASHINGTON

The Reverend Jeffrey Smith believes that theology and good food are inseparable — and he's proved it in his career as a Methodist minister, cooking instructor, and proprietor of both The Chaplain's Pantry, a gourmet food shop, and The Chaplain's Judicial Annex restaurant. As public television's Frugal Gourmet, the former University of Puget Sound chaplain liberally sprinkles his culinary demonstrations with lighthearted proverbs and quotations from the Scriptures.

This dish is best made with homemade beef stock, but you may substitute canned beef broth if necessary, which makes it an easily prepared version of a classic.

2 or 3 slices of bacon

3 pounds beef stew meat

2 to 3 cups Burgundy or other dry red wine

2 cups beef stock or canned beef broth

2 tablespoons tomato paste

3 cloves garlic, crushed

Pinch of thyme

1 bay leaf

Salt to taste

1 pound fresh mushrooms, sliced

2 or 3 yellow onions, chopped

Butter

Cut the bacon in small strips and blanch it in boiling water. Pat it dry and fry it gently, being careful not to burn the bacon or darken the fat. Remove the bacon and set it aside. Brown the stew meat in the fat quickly until it is deep brown on all sides. If you need more fat, add a little oil.

Put the meat in a 4-quart oven-proof casserole. Add the wine and stock to barely cover, and the tomato paste, garlic, thyme, bay leaf, and bacon bits. Deglaze the frying pan with a little more wine and add this liquid to the casserole. Cover the casserole.

Bake in a preheated 350° oven for 2 to 3 hours, until the meat is tender, or cook it in a heavy kettle on top of the stove.

Brown the mushrooms and onions in butter and add them to the casserole. Cook for another 20 minutes. If you like, thicken the stew with a roux.

Serve with cooked vegetables and a big salad.

Stuffed Boned Leg of Lamb   *Serves 6*
MANGIA, WEST LOS ANGELES

With Twentieth Century–Fox and MGM in the neighborhood, Kathleen Ellsworth's Mangia attracts more than its share of producers and scriptwriters and film stars at lunchtime. At that time of day they enjoy the peaceful ambiance of her little garden restaurant. And at night, when they leave the studio, they often stop in again to pick up a gourmet dish to serve to unexpected guests. This stuffed, boned leg of lamb is excellent for a small dinner party.

1 leg of lamb, 5 to 6 pounds
   when boned
2½ pounds fresh spinach,
   washed and trimmed
Just enough virgin olive oil to
   sauté the spinach

2 cups pine nuts, toasted
3 or 4 cloves garlic, crushed
   and moistened with a little
   olive oil
Salt and freshly ground black
   pepper to taste

Sauté the spinach lightly in as little olive oil as possible. While it is cooking, drip the crushed-garlic-and-olive-oil mixture onto it. Add the pine nuts and mix. Set aside.

Trim the fat and gristle away from the lamb leg, flatten it, and butterfly the left flap to make it longer. Season with salt and pepper.

Spread the lamb with the spinach mixture. Roll it up like a jelly roll and tie it with string, tighter at the ends than in the middle. Season with salt and pepper. Roast the lamb in a preheated 400° oven for approximately 50 minutes, or until the internal temperature is 110° to 120°. When it is served, the lamb should be pink.

Picadillo *Serves 4*
McMEAD'S, MIAMI, FLORIDA

John Mack was a telephone company executive in New York; Mack McMillin was in advertising with *Geo* magazine; Jim Meade was in advertising with *Gentleman's Quarterly.* They all grew tired of New York in winter and moved to the sunnier climate of Miami, where they now operate two stylish gourmet take-out shops. *Picadillo* is a sweet-sour dish from Cuba, with special touches added at McMead's.

¾ pound ground beef
¼ pound ground pork
1 medium onion, chopped
1 medium green pepper, diced
1 medium red pepper, diced
Sufficient olive oil for sautéing
½ cup green olives
½ cup raisins
1 cup beef stock

Garlic, salt, and pepper to taste
1½ cups crushed fresh or canned tomatoes
1 fresh chili pepper, chopped
½ teaspoon ground cumin
¼ teaspoon ground cloves
1 bay leaf
Dash of ground cinnamon

Sauté the ground meat, onions, and green and red peppers in a little olive oil until the meat is no longer pink and the onions are transparent. Add the rest of the ingredients and simmer for 20 minutes. Serve with rice and a salad.

Lamb and Artichoke Stew

Serves 10 to 12

THE CHAPLAIN'S PANTRY, TACOMA, WASHINGTON

"Artichokes and mushrooms are proof that God wants us to be happy," says the Reverend Jeffrey Smith, proprietor of this shop with an unusual name. "We could have gotten along without them — but who would want to?" Artichokes add a special touch to this lamb stew.

4 tablespoons butter
2 pounds boneless lamb (preferably leg), cubed
3 yellow onions, chopped
2 cloves garlic, crushed
Handful of chopped parsley
Salt and freshly ground black pepper to taste

1 6-ounce can tomato paste
1 cup dry white wine
2 cans artichoke hearts in brine, drained
½ teaspoon dried dill weed
3 tablespoons fresh lemon juice

Melt the butter in a very large skillet. Add the lamb and sauté until it is light brown. Remove the lamb and set aside. To the skillet add the onions, garlic, and parsley, and sauté briefly. Put the meat and the sautéed vegetables in a large kettle. Add the salt, pepper, tomato paste, and wine. Simmer, with the cover ajar, for about 1½ hours, or until the lamb is tender. Add the artichokes, dill weed, and lemon juice. Simmer for a few more minutes and serve over pilaf.

NEUMAN & BOGDONOFF

Moroccan Kefta

Serves 6 to 8

FÊTE ACCOMPLIE, WASHINGTON, D.C.

The food editor of the *Washington Post* called Fête Accomplie "the place to buy the kind of home cooking you wish all your hosts would serve at dinner parties." This is a doubly handy dish because it can be served with toothpicks as an hors d'oeuvre, or over rice as a main dish.

Meatballs

2 pounds ground lamb
1 cup minced onions
3 tablespoons chopped fresh
    mint (or 1 tablespoon dried)
½ cup bread crumbs
2 eggs
1 tablespoon cumin
1 teaspoon grated fresh or
    powdered ginger
½ teaspoon ground cinnamon
½ teaspoon cayenne
½ teaspoon allspice
4 cloves garlic, minced

Sauce

1 tablespoon oil
1 cup onions
2 cloves garlic, minced
1 teaspoon cumin
Pinch of ground ginger
Pinch of cayenne
1 28-ounce can Italian
    tomatoes, puréed

Combine all the meatball ingredients and mix well. Form into 1-inch balls. Poach the balls gently, in a single layer, in water for 10 minutes. Remove with a slotted spoon and set aside.

To make the sauce: Brown the onions in the oil. Add the garlic and spices and cook for 2 to 3 minutes. Add the tomatoes and simmer for 10 to 15 minutes.

Add the parboiled meatballs to the sauce and simmer for 10 minutes.

Lamb Curry with Eggplant

THE MARKET OF THE COMMISSARY, PHILADELPHIA

Serves 3

To the downtown lunchtime scene of streetcorner vendors selling hot pretzels and coffee (in Philadelphia, the pretzels are always eaten with mustard), the Commissary was the first restaurant to introduce the idea of *fine* fast food. And now stockbrokers and other busy office workers who still prefer to eat at their desks have The Market, which sells delicious take-out dishes along with a selection of groceries and fine produce.

You can, of course, vary the spiciness of this curry by using more or less of the Thai curry paste (which is available at Oriental food shops).

2 tablespoons butter
2 tablespoons flour
1 cup milk
¾ teaspoon salt
6 tablespoons corn oil
3 cups eggplant peeled and cut into ½-inch cubes
½ ounce (2½ teaspoons) red or green Thai curry paste
2 tablespoons sugar
2 tablespoons soy sauce

2 teaspoons minced garlic
2 teaspoons minced fresh ginger
2 teaspoons chopped coriander or ½ teaspoon dried coriander
12 ounces thinly sliced, well trimmed raw lamb (from shoulder or leg)
¼ cup toasted pecan halves (optional)

Melt the butter, blend in the flour, and cook for 1 minute. Whisk in the hot milk and ¼ teaspoon of the salt and whisk over low heat until the sauce thickens and bubbles. Set aside.

Heat ¼ cup of the corn oil in a skillet or a wok and add ¼ teaspoon salt and the eggplant. Cook it, stirring, over high heat for 4 to 5 minutes. Transfer to a bowl and set aside.

103

In the same pan, heat the remaining 2 tablespoons of corn oil and stir in the packet of curry paste, the sugar, and the soy sauce. Cook and stir for 1 or 2 minutes. Add the garlic, ginger, and coriander, and cook, stirring constantly, for 1 more minute. Add the lamb and the remaining ¼ teaspoon of salt, if desired, and cook, stirring constantly, for 3 to 4 minutes over high heat. Stir in the reserved sauce and the eggplant and heat through. Stir in the pecan halves, if desired.

Serve with rice and sweet-and-sour cucumbers (page 160).

Baked Veal Marden *Serves 5 or 6*

A LA CARTE AT GILLIEWRINKLES, COLD SPRING HARBOR, LONG ISLAND

As long as you don't overcook it to begin with, this rich and glamorous veal stew reheats very successfully. It also freezes well. Colorful and delicious accompaniments are a watercress salad, rice brightened with touches of chopped parsley and chives, and a little chopped onion lightly cooked in plenty of butter.

½ to 1 cup butter

2 pounds good light veal stew meat cut into 1½-inch cubes

1 medium onion, finely chopped

1 clove garlic, minced

2 10½-ounce cans condensed beef bouillon diluted with 1 can of water

1 teaspoon salt

2 bay leaves

2 5-ounce cans water chestnuts, drained

1 pound mushrooms

2 cups heavy cream

¼ teaspoon cayenne

¼ teaspoon nutmeg

¼ cup cognac

¼ cup instant-blending flour (preferably Wondra)

104

Melt ½ cup of the butter in a large skillet. Dry the veal with paper towels and brown it in the butter, a few pieces at a time. Put the meat into an oven-proof casserole with a tight-fitting lid.

Brown the onion and garlic in the same skillet, adding more butter as needed, and transfer to the casserole. Pour some of the beef broth into the pan and scrape up all of the brown bits. Add these to the casserole along with the rest of the liquid and the salt, bay leaves, and water chestnuts. Bake, covered, in a preheated 375° oven for 1¼ to 1½ hours, or until the veal is tender. Do not over-cook it.

While the veal is baking, wipe the mushrooms clean with a damp paper towel, cut off the bottoms of their stems, and quarter the mushrooms. Melt more butter in the skillet and sauté the mushrooms over fairly high heat, being careful not to crowd the pan.

With a slotted spoon, remove the veal and water chestnuts from the casserole. Bring the liquid in which they were cooked to a simmer and blend in the cream, cayenne, and nutmeg. Add the cognac. Briskly whisk in the flour a little at a time, simmering the sauce gently. If it seems too thin, add more flour; if too thick, add more cream or milk. Taste the sauce and correct the seasonings. Then add the veal, water chestnuts, and mushrooms to the sauce and stir gently.

Balducci's

Lime Veal with Kiwi

Serves 4

GOURMET PASTA, GREAT NECK, LONG ISLAND, AND
NEW YORK CITY (UPPER EAST SIDE)

Pasta is only the half of it in these two gourmet shops. Chef
Seth Pitlake prides himself on the variety of his creations and
on his personal interpretation of *nouvelle cuisine*. This veal
dish with kiwi fruit from the Pacific is a fine example.

4 large veal scallops, pounded
  thin
6 tablespoons flour
Sufficient olive oil for sautéing
½ cup dry white wine
  (preferably Chablis)
½ cup unsalted butter

Juice of 4 limes
½ teaspoon freshly ground
  white pepper
1 teaspoon fresh dill
2 limes, sliced
2 kiwi fruit, peeled and sliced

Dredge the veal in the flour and sauté in olive oil for 1 minute on
each side. Drain the veal on paper towels. Add the wine, butter,
lime juice, white pepper, and dill to the sauté pan and bring the
liquid to a boil. Let the mixture cook for 3 minutes. Add the veal
and simmer for 2 minutes. Serve garnished with the lime and kiwi
slices.

Because there is no thickener in this sauce, it can easily be
made in advance and the whole dish frozen. If this is done, it should
be thawed and then baked, uncovered, in a preheated 350° oven for
15 to 20 minutes.

Pork Roast Stuffed with Smoked Sausage

KENESSEY GOURMETS INTERNATIONALE, CHICAGO

Serves 6 to 8

Its Irish-sounding name notwithstanding, this Chicago gourmet market's owner-manager is Hungarian-born Ivan Kenessey, who came to the United States during the Hungarian revolution. He sells foods and wines of all nations in his market, but, understandably, the Hungarian dishes his chef prepares for take-out are among his own favorites.

A 6-pound loin pork roast, boned

2 cloves of garlic, slivered and inserted into slits in the roast

1 14-inch-long Hungarian hot smoked sausage (or Polish or Portuguese hot smoked sausage)

1 onion, chopped

1 stalk celery, sliced

1 carrot, sliced

2 bay leaves

½ teaspoon thyme

1 cup dry white wine

1 cup water

Salt and freshly ground black pepper to taste

Using a skewer, stuff the roast with the sausage. Brown the roast in a heavy skillet or Dutch oven. Remove the roast and any excess fat. Then brown the onion, carrot, and celery in the skillet. Return the roast to the skillet and add the bay leaves, thyme, wine, and water. Cover the skillet with aluminum foil (or put the cover on the Dutch oven) and bake the roast for 2 hours in a preheated 325° oven. Transfer the roast to a platter. Degrease the braising liquid and pour it into a sauceboat. Red cabbage and boiled potatoes are the ideal accompaniment to this roast.

Pork and Apricot Stew

Serves 8

REX'S MARKET DELICATESSEN, SEATTLE

Rex McFadden fulfilled a long-time dream when he left the executive offices of Seattle's Washington Athletic Club to open his food shop at the north end of the city's famed Pike Place Public Market. With its attractive farmers' stands, fishmongers, cheese merchants, and other food suppliers, the Market provides Rex with his ingredients and his customers. This stew is a favorite with the take-out dinner trade.

3 pounds pork shoulder, cubed
4 tablespoons butter
1 pound onions, coarsely
  chopped
4 cloves garlic, minced
¼ cup flour
1½ cups cider
1 cup dark beer
½ cup water

¼ cup Dijon mustard
1 teaspoon cayenne
1 teaspoon ground cinnamon
1 teaspoon dried coriander
1 teaspoon salt
¾ cup chopped dried prunes
1½ cups chopped dried
  apricots

Place the pork pieces in one layer in a large roasting pan and brown them for 20 minutes in a preheated 350° oven.

Melt the butter in a heavy casserole or Dutch oven and sauté the onions and garlic until tender. Add the flour and cook for 3 minutes, stirring constantly. Add the pork and cook for 3 more minutes. Add the remaining ingredients and simmer the stew, uncovered, for 1½ to 2 hours, stirring occasionally, until the pork is tender.

Black Beans with Andouille Sausage

THE OAKVILLE GROCERY COMPANY,
SAN FRANCISCO

Serves 4 to 6

At San Francisco's Oakville Grocery, sausages come in more than two hundred varieties — New Orleans *andouille,* flavored with garlic and cayenne, among them. This bean-and-sausage dish, invented by chef Kathleen Lewis, may be served either as a hot casserole or as a cold salad.

1 pound black beans, soaked
  overnight and drained
Water to cover
2 bay leaves
2 whole garlic cloves, peeled
1 whole yellow onion, peeled
1 whole carrot, peeled
1 whole stalk celery
1 pound *andouille* sausage (or
  kielbasa or chorizo)

1 red onion, diced
1 red pepper, diced
1 green pepper, diced
1 to 3 jalapeño peppers, fresh
  or canned, minced
2 garlic cloves, minced
Salt and freshly ground black
  pepper to taste

To the beans and water, add the bay leaves and whole vegetables. Bring the liquid to a boil, cover the pot, reduce the heat, and simmer for 1½ to 2 hours, until the beans are tender. Remove the vegetables from the beans. Make sure there is about ½ inch of liquid above the beans, and add more water at this point if there is not. Add the whole sausage, as well as the onion, peppers, and garlic. Season with salt and pepper, and simmer for 30 minutes. Remove the sausage. Dice it and return it to the pot. Adjust the seasonings. Serve hot with sour cream and sliced green onions on top.

    To serve the beans as a cold salad, add 1 cup of vinaigrette made with ⅓ cup vinegar, ⅔ cup oil, 1 tablespoon Dijon mustard, and salt and pepper to the beans while they are still hot. Let them cool to room temperature.

Rabbit with Apricots
Serves 8 to 10

LE PETIT CHEF, MINNEAPOLIS

Jean-Claude Tindillier started his gourmet take-out shop with a loyal following from his days as chef of the French restaurant Chouette. Among the most loyal customers, surely, is the one from Iowa who regularly sends his plane to the Twin Cities to pick up one or another special treat for a dinner party.

A panel of eight, invited by a local newspaper to sample the offerings at Le Petit Chef, unanimously voted this the best entrée.

2 rabbits (about 2½ pounds each)
¾ cup cider vinegar
2 cups red wine (preferably Cabernet Sauvignon)
4 unpeeled garlic cloves
2 bay leaves
2 stalks celery, cut up

½ teaspoon thyme
2 sprigs parsley
2 cups dried apricots
⅓ cup peanut oil
½ cup butter
Salt and freshly ground black pepper to taste
2 teaspoons sugar

Bone the rabbits and cut the meat into bite-size pieces. Marinate them overnight in the refrigerator in a mixture of the vinegar, wine, garlic cloves, bay leaves, celery, thyme, and parsley.

Soak the apricots for 2 hours in cold water. Drain and set aside.

Remove the pieces of rabbit from the marinade and drain them well. Reserve the marinade.

In a large Dutch oven, sauté the rabbit pieces in the oil and butter. Season them with salt and pepper and brown them on all sides. Pour off the fat.

Sprinkle the meat with the sugar and cook until the pieces are nicely browned and carmelized. Add the marinade and the apricots. Cook slowly, covered, for 45 minutes to 1 hour, until the meat is thoroughly cooked.

Remove the garlic, celery, bay leaves, and parsley from the sauce. Peel and crush the garlic cloves and return them to the sauce. Strain the sauce.

Place the rabbit pieces and the apricots on a platter and pour the sauce over all. Serve very hot.

Le Petit Chef

Choucroute Garnie *Serves 8*
DEMARCHELIER, NEW YORK CITY (UPPER EAST SIDE)

This Alsatian specialty is a popular winter dish with customers of Demarchelier. These include fashion designer Ralph Lauren and actresses Candice Bergen, Sophia Loren, and Diana Ross. Most of the ingredients for this recipe can be found in German butcher shops.

4 pounds sauerkraut

2 tablespoons goose, duck, or pork fat

2 medium carrots, sliced

1 onion stuck with cloves

8 slices bacon

2 cups beef broth (may be made from bouillon cubes)

12 juniper berries

3 pounds smoked pork butt, sliced into eight pieces

1 smoked goose leg

8 frankfurters

8 Kassler ribs (cooked smoked rack or roast of pork), sliced

Boiled potatoes for garnish (optional)

Rinse the sauerkraut thoroughly in a colander and set it aside.

Put the goose fat, carrots, onion, and bacon into a large stockpot and fry them over medium heat for 5 to 10 minutes, until the carrots are soft. Be sure not to brown the onion. Add the drained sauerkraut and the beef broth and enough water to cover. Add the juniper berries and bring the liquid to a boil. Cook for 1 hour over medium heat.

Add the sliced pork and the goose leg and cook for another hour over medium heat. Lower the flame and simmer for another 30 minutes.

Add the frankfurters and sliced Kassler ribs. Simmer for 10 to 15 minutes. Keep the flame low, or the frankfurters will break up.

Serve the *choucroute* on a large platter with the sauerkraut underneath and the assorted *charcuterie* on top. Garnish with boiled potatoes, if desired.

marché Gourmet

Salads

Curried Shrimp and Rice Salad   *Serves 8*

REBECCA'S, BOSTON

On weekend mornings, the young residents of Beacon Hill flock down to Rebecca's for croissants and coffee. Weekdays, on their way home from work, they stop in for entrées to take up the hill for dinner. Rebecca Caras comes from a family of restaurateurs, and has a good idea of the styles of cooking her customers want. In her salads, there are always plenty of crunchy vegetables. Her cakes are rich and moist, her pâtés imaginative. This simple salad is a long-standing favorite.

Salad

2 cups cooked white rice
½ cup sliced green stuffed
   olives
1 cup chopped green pepper

¼ cup thinly sliced scallions
¼ cup capers
1 pound cooked small shrimp

Dressing

2 cups mayonnaise
2 tablespoons curry powder

Juice of half a lemon
Salt and freshly ground black
   pepper to taste

Mix all the salad ingredients together. Combine the dressing ingredients and add to the salad. Toss well to combine evenly.

Mexican Shrimp Salad

Serves 6 to 8

JIM JAMAIL & SONS FOOD MARKET, HOUSTON

This is a gloriously colorful salad, a reminder that Mexico is a next-door neighbor to Texas.

1 medium red onion
1 green pepper
1 red pepper
3 medium tomatoes, seeded and juiced
1½ pounds medium shrimp, cooked, peeled, and deveined
½ cup pitted black olives, cut in half (reserve ½ cup of juice from the can)
½ cup stuffed green olives, cut in half

½ cup olive oil
⅓ cup lemon juice
1 clove garlic, finely minced
1 teaspoon cumin
1 bay leaf, crushed
1 jalapeño pepper, fresh or pickled, finely minced
Salt and freshly ground black pepper to taste
2 lemons, thinly sliced (for garnish)

Cut the onions, peppers, and tomatoes into julienne strips and place in a bowl. Add the shrimp and the olives.

Combine the remaining ingredients (including the olive liquid) except the lemons. Pour the dressing over the shrimp and vegetables. Toss well to mix, and refrigerate for several hours. Garnish with the lemon slices.

Seafood Pasta Salad

Serves 6

WASHINGTON MARKET, NEW YORK CITY (TRIBECA)

What Dean & DeLuca is to SoHo, the Washington Market is to Tribeca, the even-farther-downtown Manhattan area of high lofts and converted warehouses that is on the upswing. The site of this shop is one of the original buildings of the old Washington Market, once the city's wholesale food district. This handsome high-ceilinged building, which originally housed a store that sold soda syrup, has six-foot aisles. If you want to bring down a crowd to dance, you can hire a jazz trio and order a buffet. Meanwhile, back in your own kitchen, here's one of the market's most popular pasta salads.

1 pound pasta, preferably *penne* or ziti

½ cup olive oil

½ pound medium shrimp

½ pound sea scallops

2½ cups court bouillon or 2 cups bottled clam juice and ½ cup dry white vermouth

12 mussels

½ pound cooked lobster meat (optional)

Pinch of cayenne

Salt and freshly ground black pepper to taste

2 cups mayonnaise, preferably homemade

Julienne strips of pimiento (for garnish)

Cook the pasta in boiling salted water until it is done. Drain it thoroughly and coat it with olive oil. Set aside.

Place the shrimp in a saucepan and cover with cold water. Bring the water to a boil and turn off the heat. Let the shrimp sit in the water for 2 minutes. Drain, shell, and devein the shrimp; cut them into 1-inch pieces and add to the pasta.

116

Rinse the scallops. Bring the court bouillon to a simmer. Add the scallops and poach for 5 minutes. Drain the scallops and cut them into two or three slices each. Add to the pasta.

Clean and scrub the mussels thoroughly. Steam until the shells open. (Discard any that do not open.) Add the mussels to the pasta, reserving the shells for garnish.

Cut the lobster meat into 1-inch chunks and add to the pasta.

Add the cayenne, salt, and pepper to the mayonnaise and stir it into the salad. Chill.

To serve, garnish with the pimiento strips and reserved mussel shells.

Curried Crab Meat   *Serves 6*
LES CHEFETTES, GREAT NECK, LONG ISLAND

This is a flavorful filling for artichoke bottoms, tomatoes, or avocados — a lovely lunch dish.

½ pound fresh, frozen, or
    canned crab meat
1 tablespoon minced scallions
½ tablespoon lemon juice

¼ teaspoon dry mustard
3 tablespoons mayonnaise
1 teaspoon curry powder
1 teaspoon dry sherry

Mix all ingredients well and stuff your choice of vegetables. You may also use this as a stuffing for hors d'oeuvres.

Lobster Salad

Serves 4 to 6

THE BLACK FOREST, CAMBRIDGE

Richard Silver and his partner Marge DeMeyere built The Black Forest literally with their own hands. When their catering business outgrew Richard's apartment, they rented the cellar of the Cambridge Country Store. Nine hundred sixty-three cinder blocks later, they had a working kitchen with two walk-in refrigerators. Later, with the addition of showcases and small red-clothed tables, The Black Forest expanded into a take-out store and cheerful eatery. Although it's still hidden away at the bottom of a steep flight of stairs, word of mouth has quickly made this into one of the most popular gourmet shops in Cambridge.

Obviously this salad is for a special occasion.

2 ounces dried Chinese black mushrooms
¼ pound snow pea pods
1 pound cooked lobster meat

3 tablespoons soy sauce
½ cup vinaigrette dressing (see recipe below)
1 head Boston lettuce

Put the mushrooms in boiling water and let them soak for 20 minutes. Remove the stems and cut the caps into julienne strips. Pick off the ends of the pea pods. Dice the lobster meat into 1-inch chunks.

Combine the mushrooms, pea pods, and lobster pieces in a bowl and toss with the soy sauce and the vinaigrette. Chill. Serve on leaves of Boston lettuce.

Vinaigrette Dressing

¾ cup olive oil
¼ cup wine vinegar
1 teaspoon Dijon mustard
1 clove garlic, minced

Pinch of thyme
Salt and freshly ground black
   pepper to taste

Combine all the ingredients in a jar with a tight cover, and shake well.

Smoked Whitefish Salad
Serves 2 or 3

E.A.T., NEW YORK CITY (UPPER EAST SIDE)

Selling food was not the life Eli Zabar envisioned for himself when he was majoring in medieval history at Columbia. But when he sold out his share of his father's famous West Side delicatessen, it was to set up an East Side food emporium for himself. Well, actually, not for himself — E.A.T. stands for Eli and Abbie Together. Abbie is his designer wife, the person generally credited with starting the gourmet food shop look: white tile walls, stainless steel counters, and natural butcher-block shelves, a mix that symbolizes homeyness and dazzling chic. Still, Eli obviously hasn't forgotten his background. This smoked whitefish salad would be as at home at Zabar's as it is at E.A.T.

1 cup flaked smoked whitefish
   (or Indian-style salmon or
   any other smoked white
   moist flaky fish)

Juice of half a lemon
¼ cup mayonnaise
¼ cup chopped red onions

Mash the fish. Add the lemon juice, and mix in the mayonnaise. Sprinkle with the chopped onions.

119

Seafood Salad

Serves 6 to 8

THE AMERICAN CAFÉ MARKET, WASHINGTON, D.C.

As an eighteen-year-old business administration student at Georgetown University, Bob Giamo missed the kind of sandwiches he grew up on in New York. With two friends, also in their teens, he raised $20,000 and opened a Blimpie franchise in Georgetown. Five years later, Giamo, Jim Sullivan, and Mark Caraluzzi closed down their fast-food sandwich shop and opened their first American Café. It was a gastronomical leap that has paid off handsomely. Today there are three cafés, each with its Market for specialty foods and carry-out cuisine. The branch on Capitol Hill and the one in Baltimore are serviced from the main kitchen in Georgetown.

5 cups water

1½ cups beer

1 lemon, sliced

4 tablespoons shrimp boil (see recipe below)

1½ pounds squid, cleaned and cut into ¼-to-½-inch rings

1 pound bay scallops (or sea scallops, cut up)

½ pound whole shrimp, peeled and deveined

1 bell pepper, diced

⅓ cup finely chopped parsley

1 teaspoon oregano

3 scallions, sliced

Dressing (see recipe below)

Bring the water and beer to a boil. Add the lemon slices and shrimp boil and reduce the heat to low. Simmer for 10 minutes.

Add the squid to the water and poach for 12 to 15 minutes. Add the shrimp and poach for another 5 minutes. Add the scallops and poach for another 3 minutes.

120

Drain the seafood and plunge it into very cold water for 1 minute. Dry the pieces well, patting them between paper towels. Put them in a bowl and add the bell pepper, parsley, oregano, and scallions. Add the dressing, and mix well. Serve at room temperature.

Shrimp Boil

⅓ to 1 tablespoon yellow mustard seeds

3 tablespoons coriander seeds

1 tablespoon red pepper flakes

1 tablespoon chopped bay leaves

¼ teaspoon dill seeds

10 seeds allspice

2 whole cloves

1 tablespoon kosher salt

Combine all the ingredients. This recipe will make enough seasoning for 2 pounds of shrimp. Store it in a tightly sealed jar and use it another time to cook shrimp for cocktail.

Dressing

½ cup lemon juice

Zest of 1 lemon

1 teaspoon salt

½ teaspoon freshly ground black pepper

1½ teaspoons chopped garlic

⅔ cup olive oil

Put all the ingredients except the olive oil in a bowl or a blender. Slowly add the oil while whisking or blending at high speed until it is all incorporated.

Squid Salad with Vegetables

THE FISHMONGER, CAMBRIDGE

If the word *fishmonger* conjures up an image of a Dickensian character hawking his newspaper-wrapped wares from a dingy stall, meet Dorothy Borden. This fishmonger is a strikingly attractive young mother and her shop is a cheerful, brightly lit store filled with displays of fresh, fresh fish and with the aromas of fish dishes being prepared for her take-out trade. A shelf of cookbooks is available for browsing, and Dorothy enjoys introducing her customers to new and unfamiliar varieties of seafood, including squid, which you can now find in many fish markets. You no longer have to go to Italy to eat *calamari.*

1¾ pounds (about 4 cups) cleaned and cut up squid

6 quarts water

1 teaspoon salt

¼ cup lemon juice

⅔ to ¾ cup thinly sliced green pepper

2 large carrots, cut into julienne matchsticks

3 stalks celery, cut into julienne matchsticks

1 cup thinly sliced red onion

3 tablespoons finely chopped parsley

½ cup olive oil

¼ cup red wine vinegar

¼ cup lemon juice

Grated rind of 1 lemon

1 clove garlic, minced

2 tablespoons fresh or frozen basil, finely chopped

1 teaspoon salt

½ teaspoon freshly ground black pepper

Bring the water to a boil. Add the salt and lemon juice. Drop the squid pieces into the water and check them after a minute or two. When the edges curl, they are done. Taste a piece to be sure, but don't let them overcook, since overcooked squid is very chewy.

Drain the squid immediately and plunge them into a bowl of ice water. When they are thoroughly chilled, drain them well and put them in a large bowl in the refrigerator.

Add the green pepper, carrots, celery, red onion, and parsley to the bowl with the squid.

Blend the olive oil, vinegar, ¼ cup lemon juice, lemon rind, garlic, basil, and salt and pepper in a blender or food processor. Add the vinaigrette dressing to the bowl of squid and vegetables and toss well. Serve very cold.

Pesto Tortellini   *Serves 6 to 8*

THE BLACK FOREST, CAMBRIDGE

Tortellini salads are the most "in" of the cold pasta salads. Chef Richard Silver recommends this dish because, aside from being delicious, it is inexpensive, filling, and splendid-looking.

2 pounds tortellini
2 plum tomatoes, fresh (in season) or canned
¼ pound Abruzzi sausages, or pepperoni

½ cup whole almonds
½ cup pesto (see recipe below)

Cook the tortellini according to directions on the package. Drain and rinse, and drain again. Cut the tomatoes into eighths. Slice the sausage thinly.

Combine the tortellini, sausages, tomatoes, and almonds. While the pasta is still warm, toss with the pesto sauce. Chill. Serve cold or at room temperature.

Pesto

1 cup fresh basil
¼ cup olive oil
1 large clove garlic, minced
1½ tablespoons walnuts

¼ cup grated Parmesan cheese
2 tablespoons ricotta
Salt, if desired

Blend the basil, olive oil, garlic, and walnuts in a blender or food processor. Fold in the Parmesan and ricotta cheeses and taste for salt.

Spiral Pasta Salad
Serves 10

DEMARCHELIER, NEW YORK CITY (UPPER EAST SIDE)

Paris-born Eric Demarchelier opened his gourmet take-out shop under the influence of his fashion photographer brother Patrick. Not surprisingly, fashion models figure prominently among the shop's clientele.

This salad may be varied by adding chunks of cheese, steamed broccoli, cauliflower, or string beans, or lightly cooked peas.

½ pound spiral egg pasta
½ pound spiral tomato egg pasta
½ pound spiral spinach egg pasta
½ pound spiral whole-wheat pasta
1 cup fresh basil leaves, chopped

1 egg yolk
2 tablespoons Dijon mustard
3 tablespoons red wine vinegar
2 tablespoons peanut or corn oil
¼ cup water
Salt and freshly ground black pepper to taste

124

Cook the pasta in salted boiling water and drain in a colander under running cold water. Set the pasta and basil aside while you prepare the dressing.

Combine the egg yolk, mustard, and vinegar, beating vigorously with a wire whisk. Slowly add the oil, beating until the dressing has the consistency of mayonnaise. When all the oil has been incorporated, beat in the water slowly with the whisk. Add the salt and pepper. Combine the pasta, basil, and dressing and toss well. Serve at room temperature.

Santorini Salad
Serves 6 to 8

PRIME CONCERN, GREAT NECK, LONG ISLAND

Even though the Greek island of Santorini is rocky and volcanic, its population has long managed to produce both fine grapes for sweet wines and a variety of vegetables. This salad of crisp cucumbers and juicy tomatoes makes use of some of the island's produce.

1 pound ziti, cooked
½ cup chopped fresh basil
2 large cucumbers, cut into chunky slices
4 large tomatoes, cut into eighths

¾ pound feta cheese, cubed
½ cup corn oil
½ cup vinegar
Salt and freshly ground black pepper to taste

Toss the ziti, basil, cucumbers, tomatoes, and feta cheese together. Add the oil and vinegar and the salt and pepper. Toss again. Serve chilled or at room temperature.

Mussel and Pasta Salad

THE FISHMONGER, CAMBRIDGE

In Cambridge, you can buy all the ingredients for this salad in three adjoining specialty food shops on Huron Avenue — the mussels at The Fishmonger, the pasta and cheese at Formaggio Kitchen, and the vegetables (as well as flowers for the table) at Le Jardin. Within the past few years, this neighborhood — a mix of Boston Brahmins, Harvard professors, students, and young professionals — has been enlivened by these attractive food shops.

2 pounds mussels
1 bay leaf
Pinch of thyme
Handful of chopped parsley stems (if available)
½ pound pasta shells
½ pound mushrooms, quartered
2 tablespoons butter
Salt and freshly ground black pepper to taste
½ medium red pepper, diced
½ medium green pepper, diced
1 clove garlic, minced
2 tablespoons finely chopped parsley

½ cup plus 2 tablespoons olive oil
Juice of half a lemon plus enough red wine vinegar to equal ¼ cup
Rind of half a lemon, finely grated
¼ cup Parmesan cheese, finely grated
1½ tablespoons Pommery mustard
¼ teaspoon salt
¼ teaspoon freshly ground black pepper

Wash the mussels and pull off the "beards."

Put the bay leaf, thyme, and parsley stems into a large pot with a lid. Put about ½ inch of water in the pot and bring it to a boil with the lid on. When the water is boiling hard, throw the mussels in quickly and put the lid back on. Steam the mussels for about 5 minutes, until the shells open. (Discard any that do not open.) Drain the mussels and save the broth for another use. It may be frozen.

Shell the mussels. Put them in a large bowl and refrigerate.

Cook the pasta shells until *al dente.* Drain them and plunge them into cold water. When they are cooled, drain them very well and add them to the bowl in the refrigerator.

Sauté the mushrooms in the butter until they are brown. Season with salt and pepper to taste and let them cool.

Add the cooled mushrooms and the diced peppers to the bowl in the refrigerator.

Put the minced garlic and chopped parsley in a bowl and chop it together. Add the remaining ingredients and whisk well. Add this dressing to the salad and toss lightly so as not to mash the mussels. Check for seasonings. Serve cold.

Pasta Primavera

Serves 4 to 6 as an entrée

GRETCHEN'S OF COURSE, SEATTLE

A few years ago, Gretchen Mathers left a post as an executive with a hotel and food conglomerate to open her own take-out shop and catering service. It wasn't long before her enterprise burgeoned into a restaurant where passers-by could watch Gretchen at work, and now she has a second outlet for her products at Jack's Fish Spot, one of Seattle's specialty seafood markets.

1 pound linguini, preferably fresh
1 10-ounce package frozen peas
1 pound fresh broccoli
3 ounces pimientos, chopped
½ cup chopped parsley

1½ to 2 cups grated Parmesan cheese
1 to 1½ cups half-and-half
1½ teaspoons salt, or to taste
½ teaspoon freshly ground black pepper

Cut the linguini into 6-inch lengths. In 4 to 6 quarts of rapidly boiling salted water, cook fresh pasta for about 2 minutes, dried according to package directions. Do not overcook. Drain the pasta and rinse it with cold water until cool. Put the peas in a colander and run water over them to thaw. Cut the broccoli into flowerets and blanch them in boiling water for 1 to 2 minutes. Combine all the ingredients in a large bowl and mix them together gently but thoroughly.

Sesame Noodle Salad

Serves 6 to 8

THE AMERICAN CAFÉ MARKET, WASHINGTON, D.C.

This salad was rated "marvelous" by a *Washington Post* reviewer. Be sure to follow the directions for cooking and draining the pasta exactly, or the salad will be pasty.

1 tablespoon salt
1 pound linguini, fettuccine, or thin spaghetti
¼ cup sesame oil
3 tablespoons soy sauce or tamari

¼ teaspoon black pepper
½ sweet red pepper, diced very fine
¼ cup chopped watercress leaves
½ teaspoon chopped garlic

Bring 4 quarts of water to a boil with the salt. Drop in the pasta and cook it for 3 minutes after the water returns to a boil.

Drain the pasta quickly and submerge it in cold water for about 30 seconds. Drain off the water, tossing the pasta to get rid of as much moisture as possible.

Put the pasta in a large bowl and immediately stir in the sesame oil, soy sauce, and pepper. Mix in the remaining ingredients.

Refrigerate the salad, preferably overnight. Serve it cold.

129

Cheese Tortellini

Serves 4 to 6

FORMAGGIO KITCHEN, CAMBRIDGE

Cheese tortellini can be found in many supermarkets as well as specialty shops.

1 pound cheese tortellini
⅓ cup olive oil
2 cups fresh vegetables, diced
(Use any combination of
zucchini, broccoli, yellow
squash, green peppers, and
tomatoes. Blanch all the
vegetables except the
tomatoes.)

½ cup grated Parmesan cheese
4 tablespoons chopped parsley
Freshly ground black pepper to
taste
Julienne strips of salami
(optional)

Cook the tortellini in a large amount of rapidly boiling salted water until they rise to the top. Drain but do not rinse. Transfer the tortellini to a warm bowl and toss with olive oil until they are well coated. Add the vegetables, Parmesan cheese, and chopped parsley. Mix together and season with freshly ground pepper. Garnish with salami if you like. Serve at room temperature.

Straw and Hay Salad

Serves 6 to 8

marché GOURMET, SCOTTSDALE, ARIZONA

These days, no elegant shopping center is complete without its gourmet food shop, and The Borgata, with its Renaissance-inspired courtyards and fifty select shops and restaurants, is no exception. Cold pasta salad with an American Southwest name seems singularly appropriate here.

½ pound spinach fettuccine
½ pound regular fettuccine
1½ cups olive oil
⅓ cup tarragon vinegar
1 pound Genoa salami, cut in
 julienne strips
2 cups grated Parmesan cheese

3 ounces black olives, chopped
2 tablespoons fresh thyme
2 tablespoons fresh basil
2 tablespoons fresh oregano
Pinch of rosemary
Salt and freshly ground black
 pepper to taste

Cook the fettuccine according to directions on the package. Drain and set aside to cool. Mix the oil and vinegar together in a large bowl. Stir in the remaining ingredients. Add the fettuccine and mix well. Refrigerate overnight.

Mediterranean Pasta Salad   Serves 5 or 6
THE FRUIT LADY, PHILADELPHIA

This salad is very good as a leftover. Save about one third of the dressing to refresh the salad the second time around.

1 pound rotini spirals, cooked
 al dente
1 head broccoli flowerets,
 blanched and refreshed in
 cold water
1 can white tuna in water,
 drained and chopped
1½ red peppers, diced

4 tablespoons capers
4 tablespoons red wine vinegar
1 clove garlic
½ tablespoon oregano
½ tablespoon salt
¾ teaspoon freshly ground
 black pepper
¾ cup olive oil

Put the pasta, broccoli, tuna, and red peppers in a bowl.
   To make the vinaigrette, purée all the remaining ingredients except the oil in a blender or food processor. Then add the oil slowly, continuing to blend.
   Cover the vegetables and pasta with dressing and toss.

Orzo Salad

Serves 8

REBECCA'S, BOSTON

It was in Cambridge that Rebecca's gourmet take-out shop began a few years ago, but it blossomed and had to move to
larger quarters in Boston, at the foot of charming old Beacon
Hill. Orzo salad is one of Rebecca Caras's standbys.

2 cups raw orzo (a rice-shaped
  pasta)
1 cup feta cheese, crumbled
⅔ cup minced fresh parsley
⅔ cup minced fresh basil or
  dill

3 seeded tomatoes, coarsely
  chopped
¼ cup lemon juice
⅓ cup olive oil
Salt and pepper to taste

Cook the orzo until *al dente.* Drain it and rinse it with cold water.
Add the feta, parsley, basil or dill, and tomatoes. Combine the
lemon juice, olive oil, and salt and pepper. Pour this dressing over
the salad and toss. Serve chilled.

Ziti Salad with Sausage

Serves 8 to 10

GRETCHEN'S OF COURSE, SEATTLE

This healthful, colorful salad combines textures — smooth ziti
and pimiento with crunchy zucchini and green pepper — as
well as flavors. And the smoked farmer sausage adds a homespun touch. If you cannot find farmer sausage, substitute summer sausage or, as a last resort, salami.

12 ounces ziti

2 pounds smoked, fully cooked farmer sausage links, thinly sliced

1 pound zucchini, thinly sliced

4 tomatoes, cut in wedges

1 green pepper, seeded and chopped

1 cup chopped parsley

3 ounces pimientos, chopped

Dressing (see recipe below)

Cook the ziti in 4 to 6 quarts of boiling salted water for 7 minutes, or until just tender. Drain and rinse with cold water until cool. In a large bowl, combine all the remaining ingredients and toss gently with the dressing (add the dressing in stages; you may not need all of it). Serve cold on lettuce leaves.

Dressing

1⅓ cups olive or salad oil

⅓ cup red wine vinegar

¼ teaspoon rosemary

¼ teaspoon oregano

¼ teaspoon basil

½ teaspoon salt, or to taste

¼ teaspoon freshly ground black pepper

¼ cup grated Parmesan cheese

Put all the ingredients in a small bowl and whisk until blended.

Poulet

Pasta Salad with Spinach and Feta Cheese

THE BLACK FOREST, CAMBRIDGE   *Serves 4 to 6*

This excellent cold pasta dish is easy to make and calls for
ingredients you are likely to have on hand. But don't substitute
dried basil for the fresh; use parsley instead.

1 pound spinach fettuccine or
  other spinach pasta
6 tablespoons olive oil
Salt to taste
½ pound fresh spinach, or 1
  10-ounce package frozen
  spinach

½ pound feta cheese
8 small cherry tomatoes
2 tablespoons chopped basil
¼ cup vinaigrette dressing (see
  Lobster Salad, page 118)

Cook dried pasta for 7 to 8 minutes; fresh pasta, 4 minutes. Drain,
rinse with cold water, and drain again. Toss the pasta with 3 tablespoons of olive oil and the salt.

Steam the fresh spinach, squeeze out the water, and chop (or
thaw frozen spinach and drain thoroughly). Crumble the cheese.
Cut the tomatoes in half and toss them with the basil and 3 tablespoons of olive oil.

Put all the ingredients in a bowl and toss with the vinaigrette.
Serve cold or at room temperature.

Chicken Tarragon I   *Serves 6*

BALDUCCI'S, NEW YORK CITY (GREENWICH VILLAGE)

Forty-six years ago, Maria and Louis Balducci opened a produce market in Greenwich Village. Although they expanded

and moved several times, the importance of fresh produce was always paramount. Anytime Maria Balducci found a tomato that was the least bit soft she would carry it away, shaking her head and murmuring that she really needed a kitchen in the store so she could cook things from the soft tomatoes, the broken broccoli flowerets, and the ends of spaghetti. That was the beginning of Balducci's gourmet take-out shop, today one of the largest and best known in New York City. Actresses Meryl Streep and Cicely Tyson shop there, as does singer Lena Horne, but so do neighborhood residents in need of a crisp bunch of celery. This recipe is one of Balducci's customers' favorites.

Sauce

3 stalks celery, coarsely
  chopped
2 medium carrots, coarsely
  chopped
1 medium yellow onion,
  coarsely chopped

4 tablespoons dried tarragon
2 to 3 cups chicken broth
5 black peppercorns
1½ cups mayonnaise

Combine all the ingredients except the mayonnaise in a saucepan. Bring them to a boil and cook until the vegetables are tender. Set the mixture aside to cool; then purée it in a blender. Remove the mixture to a bowl and fold in the mayonnaise.

Chicken

3 pounds boneless, skinned
  chicken breasts, seasoned

with garlic powder, salt, and
pepper

Bake the chicken breasts in a preheated 450° oven until they are completely cooked, about 20 minutes. When the chicken is cool, cut it into bite-size pieces and combine it with the sauce. Garnish with whole cherry tomatoes, marinated artichoke hearts, and strips of red pepper.

135

Chicken Tarragon II

Serves 4

THE AMERICAN CAFÉ MARKET, WASHINGTON, D.C.

Chicken salad flavored with tarragon is one of the most popular items in take-out food shops everywhere. This very easy and delicious version owes at least part of its success to the roasting of the chicken breasts.

2 whole chicken breasts
¾ cup mayonnaise
1 tablespoon fresh tarragon, chopped (or tarragon bottled in vinegar, drained)

½ teaspoon salt
¼ teaspoon freshly ground black pepper
2 tablespoons sliced blanched almonds

Roast the chicken in a preheated 350° oven for 20 to 30 minutes. Let it cool. Then pick the meat from the bone as quickly as possible.

Cut the chicken into 1-inch pieces and mix it with the remaining ingredients. Chill before serving.

Chicken and Broccoli Salad

Serves 8 to 10

GOODIES TO GO, LEXINGTON, MASSACHUSETTS

With toasted Syrian bread, herbed butter, and fresh ripe tomatoes, what could be better than this nourishing salad on a summer's day?

4 whole chicken breasts
1½ to 2 cups broccoli flowerets
1 medium red onion, diced
¾ cup chopped fresh dill

Juice of half a lemon
½ cup mayonnaise
¾ cup sour cream
Salt and freshly ground black pepper to taste

136

Poach the chicken breasts in simmering water until cooked but still tender. Let them cool.

Cook the broccoli in boiling salted water for 4 to 5 minutes. It should be crunchy. Set it aside.

Mix together the onion, dill, lemon juice, mayonnaise, sour cream, and salt and pepper. Remove the meat from the cooled chicken breasts and cut it into bite-size pieces. Add the broccoli to the chicken pieces and toss all together with the dressing. Chill the salad and serve on a bed of lettuce.

Italian Chicken Salad   Serves 6 to 8
FETTUCCINE BROS., SAN FRANCISCO

One day at lunch, Bob Battaglia and Don Woodall, young executives with a San Francisco manufacturer of backpacking equipment, were enjoying their food so much they decided to give up backpacking equipment altogether and turn to their first love — cooking. Specializing in homemade pasta, which they produce in great quantity, they also sell sauces, salads, meats, cheeses, and oven-ready dishes. Their Italian chicken salad recipe is made special by its flavorful dressing.

Dressing

1½ teaspoons lemon juice
¼ teaspoon thyme

Salt and freshly ground black pepper to taste
2 teaspoons anchovy paste

Whisk all the ingredients together and let the dressing sit at room temperature for 1 hour.

Salad

1 cup walnuts, chopped
2 tablespoons butter
10 to 12 frozen or canned
   artichoke hearts, halved
1 or 2 red peppers, cut in
   ¾-inch strips
½ cup fresh peas

1 ½ pounds chicken breasts,
   poached and cooled in their
   liquid
¾ pound fresh green beans, cut
   into 2-inch lengths, steamed
   for 3 to 4 minutes
¼ cup chopped parsley
2 or 3 green onions, chopped,
   including tops

In a large skillet, lightly sauté the walnuts in the butter. Then add the artichokes, peppers, and peas, stirring often over a low flame for 3 minutes. Remove these ingredients to a bowl. Cut the chicken into bite-size pieces and add them to the sautéed mixture. Add the remaining ingredients. Toss the salad well with the dressing. Allow it to season for an hour or so before serving. Serve at room temperature.

Oriental Chicken

Serves 3 or 4

THE BLACK FOREST, CAMBRIDGE

Asked by a client to cater a small luncheon in honor of Mimi Sheraton, food critic for the *New York Times,* Richard Silver devised an Oriental duck salad as a first course. Delicious as it was, the duck made it too expensive for his café–carry-out business, so he substituted the chicken. Since this is the single most popular salad at The Black Forest, the substitution is clearly a success.

1 pound chicken breast meat,
cooked

2 bunches scallions

2 ounces dried Chinese black
mushrooms

½ pound fresh water chestnuts,
diced (optional)

1 tablespoon soy sauce

¼ cup vinaigrette dressing (see
Lobster Salad, page 118)

Cut the chicken into julienne strips. Mince the scallions. Soak the mushrooms in hot water for 20 minutes. Remove the stems and cut the caps into julienne strips.

Combine the chicken, scallions, mushrooms, and water chestnuts and coat with the soy sauce. Toss with the vinaigrette. Serve cold or at room temperature.

Curried Chicken Salad I   *Serves 8*

SUZANNE'S, WASHINGTON, D.C.

Washington is a chicken salad town, according to Suzanne Reifers, co-owner with Judy Kahn of this appealing shop, and this curried chicken salad is one of the best.

8 whole chicken breasts,
cooked and cut into large
chunks

1 cantaloupe, cut into 1-inch
chunks

4 stalks celery, chopped

2 green apples, cut into 1-inch
chunks

Curried mayonnaise (see
recipe below)

Toasted coconut or macadamia
nuts for garnish (optional)

Combine the chicken, cantaloupe, celery, and apples in a large bowl and add the mayonnaise gradually. Chill before serving, and garnish if desired.

Curried Mayonnaise

3 egg yolks
1 cup chutney
1 cup yogurt
2 teaspoons curry powder

Juice of 2 lemons
2 cloves of garlic, minced
1 teaspoon salt or to taste
3 cups vegetable oil

Combine all the ingredients except the oil in a food processor, and blend until smooth. Add the oil slowly, continuing to blend, to form a thick mixture.

Curried Chicken Salad II   *Serves 8 to 10*
THE PUBLIC COOKSHOP, PHILADELPHIA

Deborah Baldwin and Kirk Rynearson studied together at the Restaurant School in Philadelphia and worked on a number of food-related projects before they opened their own shop. They describe their recipes as combining "our favorite things, a little Latin American, German, Chinese, Indian, northern Italian, French — a blend of international cooking."

In this recipe, the only thing that has to be cooked is the chicken.

4 cups poached chicken, cut
   into chunks
5 apples, cored and cut into
   chunks
5 stalks celery, chopped
¼ large onion, finely chopped
1 cup raisins

1 cup chopped walnuts
¼ cup brown sugar
1 tablespoon curry powder
2 cups sour cream
Juice of 3 lemons
Salt and freshly ground black
   pepper to taste

140

Put the chicken, apples, celery, onion, raisins, and walnuts in a large bowl. Combine all the remaining ingredients. Add to the salad and mix well. Taste for seasonings and adjust if necessary.

Curried Chicken Salad III   *Serves 4 to 6*
JONATHAN'S, HUNTINGTON, LONG ISLAND

When John Randall, a Long Island farmer and cheese maker and former teacher, decided to open a gourmet food emporium in 1981, he wanted it to be as much like a fine European market as possible. With its sparkling tile and marble counters and its cases filled with homemade sausages and salads and pâtés, Jonathan's does, indeed, look as if it might belong in Paris.

This curried chicken salad is an exceptionally good one for party buffets.

½ cup butter
3 tablespoons curry powder, or
    to taste
½ onion, chopped
1 cup rice
3 cups water
1 pound chicken breasts,
    skinned, boned, poached,
    and cut into bite-size pieces

1 apple, cut into ½-inch cubes
¾ cup raisins
¾ cup slivered almonds
Chopped figs and/or dates
    (optional)
2 tablespoons sugar
Salt and freshly ground black
    pepper to taste
1 cup mayonnaise

Melt the butter in a frying pan. Add the curry powder and brown it briefly. Add the onions and sauté in the curry and butter until they are soft. Sauté the rice in the curry mixture. Add the water and cover the pan. Cook until all the water has evaporated and the rice is soft but still firm.

Remove the pan from the heat. Add the chicken, fruit, and nuts to the rice mixture. Add the sugar and season with salt and pepper. Let the mixture cool. Then stir in the mayonnaise. Serve cold.

Chinese Chicken Salad *Serves 4 to 6*

MAGGIE GIN'S PURE AND FRESH CHINESE COUNTRY
COOKING RESTAURANT, ST. HELENA, CALIFORNIA

Four years ago, Maggie Gin, ski clothes designer and cookbook author, opened a Chinese country-style restaurant and take-out shop in the Napa Valley with her commercial artist husband, Bill. Here, she and her staff prepare unusual Chinese dishes as well as her special Chinese sauces — Stir-fry, Hot and Spicy, Sweet and Sour, Seafood, Five-Spice Marinade, and Pork and Rib Barbecue Sauce. Mrs. Gin bottles her sauces for distribution to gourmet food shops across the nation.

This chicken salad recipe is given its Oriental touches with hoisin sauce and sesame oil.

2 whole chicken breasts
2 tablespoons hoisin sauce
1 teaspoon Oriental sesame oil
½ cup chopped, roasted peanuts
2 scallions, finely chopped

2 tablespoons toasted sesame seeds
¼ pound *pei mei fun* (rice vermicelli), deep-fried
Lettuce
Coriander sprigs
Lemon wedges

Boil the chicken breasts for 15 minutes. When they are cool, shred the chicken with your fingers and discard the skin. Combine the shredded chicken with the hoisin sauce, sesame oil, peanuts, scallions, and sesame seeds. Toss in the fried *pei mei fun* just before serving on a bed of shredded lettuce. Garnish with coriander sprigs and lemon wedges.

Frying Pei Mei Fun

Heat peanut or corn oil as for deep-frying and add small amounts of *pei mei fun* to the hot oil. The noodles will expand immediately and rise to the surface of the oil. Remove them with a slotted spoon and let them drain on a rack.

Duck and Pheasant Salad   *Serves 6 to 8*

marché GOURMET, SCOTTSDALE, ARIZONA

> Jean Marie Rigollet and Dennis Yares preside over this European-style food market in The Borgata, a shopping center modeled on an Italian hill village. Along with fresh game, poultry, seafood, and produce, the market sells a variety of homemade foods to go, including this unusual salad.

4½- to 5-pound roast Long
   Island duckling
2- to 2¼-pound roast pheasant
2 cups mayonnaise
1 cup tart red cherries, pitted

½ cup diced celery
½ cup sliced toasted almonds
Salt and freshly ground white
   pepper to taste

When the roast birds (which should be well seasoned) are cool, separate the meat from the bones and skin. Dice it and set aside.

Put all the remaining ingredients in a large mixing bowl. Stir together and carefully mix in the diced meat. If the salad is too dry, add more mayonnaise. Serve cold.

Duck in Campari

DEAN & DeLUCA, NEW YORK CITY (SoHo)

In Lower Manhattan, some blocks away from this famous Prince Street store with its cheerfully chaotic bustle and clutter, is the gleaming, meticulously organized kitchen where the Dean & DeLuca prepared foods are cooked. Here, Peruvian-born chef Felipe Rojas-Lombardi directs his staff of "technicians" in their tall white *toques blanches* as they peel, chop, blend, and grate without the benefit of electrical kitchen gadgets. For this recipe, though, you might want to use a food processor to prepare the julienned vegetables.

2 ducks, about 5 pounds each, roasted or poached, skinned, boned, and cut into bite-size pieces
2 cups julienned celery
2 cups julienned carrots
1 cup julienned red peppers
1 cup julienned green peppers
1 cup thinly sliced scallions

2 cups mayonnaise
2 tablespoons lemon juice
3 tablespoons Campari
2 tablespoons chopped dill
3 tablespoons chopped cilantro or parsley
¼ teaspoon sugar
Salt and freshly ground black pepper to taste

Put the pieces of duck and the vegetables into a large bowl. Combine the remaining ingredients and stir this dressing into the salad. Chill.

Tabbouleh

MITCHELL COBEY CUISINE, CHICAGO

A good *tabbouleh* should be green with parsley and mint, not beige with the cracked wheat that is the essential ingredient of this Middle Eastern salad. That, at least, is the rule of Anne Serrafian, the Beirut-born chef of Mitchell Cobey Cuisine. Another of her rules is to soak the cracked wheat (also called bulgur, and available in most health food stores) in the juice from the tomatoes rather than in water.

¼ cup bulgur (cracked wheat)
5 or 6 large ripe tomatoes, seeded and chopped
3 to 4 cups chopped fresh parsley
1 cup chopped fresh mint or 2 tablespoons dried mint

1 sweet red or green pepper, chopped
1 small white onion, chopped
Juice of 3 or 4 lemons
½ cup olive oil
Salt and freshly ground black pepper to taste
A dash of cayenne

Cover the bottom of a salad bowl with the dry bulgur. Spread the chopped tomatoes over the grain so that their juice will be absorbed. Let the bulgur and tomatoes stand for about 1 hour. Then add the rest of the ingredients and mix them all together. Serve as an appetizer or a salad.

Black-Eyed Pea and Ham Salad   *Serves 6 to 8*

JIM JAMAIL & SONS FOOD MARKET, HOUSTON

Although he is German, many of chef Rolf Mietler's salads reflect the cuisine of his adopted American Southwest. This recipe calls for frozen peas and chives, but of course you can cook your own dried peas and use fresh chives if you have them.

3 10-ounce packages frozen black-eyed peas, cooked and drained (do not overcook)
2 cups diced cooked ham
½ cup tarragon wine vinegar
½ cup vegetable oil
2 ounces frozen chives
1 clove garlic, finely minced
⅓ teaspoon freshly ground white pepper
Salt to taste
4 slices crisply cooked bacon, crumbled

Put the peas and the ham in a bowl. Mix together all the other ingredients except the bacon, and pour the dressing over the salad. Toss well. Serve with the crumbled bacon on top.

THE·COMMISSARY

Vegetables
Hot and Cold

Braised Leeks with Champagne Butter Sauce

THE SILVER PALATE, NEW YORK CITY   *Serves 6*
   (UPPER WEST SIDE)

The reputation of this take-out food shop extends far beyond its own neighborhood, primarily because of the elegant packaged foods, like the champagne vinegar in this recipe, that it sells on the premises, through other shops, and by mail order.

6 medium to large leeks
7 tablespoons cold butter
2½ cups chicken stock
½ teaspoon salt

¼ teaspoon freshly ground black pepper
3 tablespoons champagne vinegar

Cut the roots and green tops off the leeks, leaving about 7 inches of the vegetable. Make a lengthwise cut 2 inches deep and wash the leeks thoroughly.

Melt 2 tablespoons of the butter in a large skillet over moderate heat and lay the leeks in the pan side by side. Pour the stock over them and sprinkle with salt and pepper.

Bring the stock to a boil and reduce the heat so the stock just simmers. Cook, uncovered, for 20 to 25 minutes, until the leeks are tender. Remove them and set them aside to keep warm.

Add the vinegar to the stock. Bring the mixture to a rapid boil, and continue cooking, stirring occasionally, until it is reduced to about 5 tablespoons.

Lower the flame and cut the remaining 5 tablespoons of butter into five pieces. Working very quickly over a very low flame, add the butter piece by piece to the reduced liquid, whisking constantly. Each piece should be incorporated before the next is added. When all the butter is incorporated, remove the skillet from the heat.

Arrange the leeks on a serving dish and drizzle the sauce over them.

Eggplant Provençal

Serves 8 to 10

GOODIES TO GO, LEXINGTON, MASSACHUSETTS

This is a good dish to prepare in advance of a party, but the Gruyère cheese must not be added until the very last minute.

3 large eggplants
Salt and freshly ground black pepper to taste
1 to 1½ pounds sweet butter
6 or 7 large onions

8 cups stewed tomatoes
1 large bunch parsley, chopped
⅓ pound Gruyère cheese, grated

Preheat oven to 350°.

Peel the eggplants and cut them into ¾-inch slices. Salt and pepper each piece and dot it with butter. Bake the eggplant on a cookie sheet for about 1 hour, until it is soft. Meanwhile, slice the onions and sauté them until soft in ¾ pound of the butter.

In another pot, simmer away the liquid from the stewed tomatoes. When they are thicker, add the parsley and the onion and continue the simmering until even thicker.

Place a layer of eggplant in a greased baking dish, cover with tomato sauce, and repeat until the eggplant and tomato sauce are gone. Top the casserole with the remaining butter and the grated Gruyère and bake it in the 350° oven until the top is brown, about 20 minutes.

If you like, you can bake the casserole without the cheese for 20 minutes early in the day. Then, just before serving, sprinkle on the grated cheese and reheat in a 350° oven for 10 to 15 minutes until the top is brown.

149

Roasted Red and Green Bell Peppers   *Serves 8*

MANGIA, WEST LOS ANGELES

Mangia is a pretty little garden restaurant and take-out shop near Twentieth Century–Fox and MGM, and it is especially popular with actors, producers, directors, and film crews. This dish is among their favorites for light luncheon dining.

4 red bell peppers
4 green bell peppers
1 large red onion
Sufficient olive oil to prevent sticking

1 cup pitted Greek olives
4 anchovy fillets
Salt and freshly ground black pepper to taste

Roast the peppers on an open flame until their skins turn black. Soak them in cold water for 20 minutes and peel under running water. It is not necessary, however, to remove all the charred skin. Cut the peppers into 1-inch-wide strips. Cut the onion into 1-inch-wide pieces. Sauté the onion in the olive oil until tender but not brown. Crush the anchovy fillets and add them, combining them with the onion well. Add the peppers and olives. Cook until *al dente*. Mix well and season with salt and pepper. Serve at room temperature.

Spanakopita   *Serves 8*

COMPLETE CUISINE LTD., ANN ARBOR

Sandi Cooper, who was trained as a developmental psychologist and once designed toys for Fisher-Price, is very education

150

oriented — which is appropriate in a town that is home to the University of Michigan. Notes in calligraphy are posted throughout her shop, explaining the products and advising customers about using them. Cooking classes are a large part of her business; and a monthly newsletter, sold by subscription, promotes her activities and those of the shop, explains such things as how champagne is made, and prints an occasional recipe. This one makes a very good luncheon dish.

2 10-ounce packages frozen chopped spinach, thawed
¾ cup chopped onions
3 eggs
¼ cup chopped scallions
¼ pound feta cheese, crumbled
1½ teaspoons dill weed
¼ cup finely chopped parsley
Salt, freshly ground black pepper, and nutmeg to taste
½ cup unsalted butter, melted
1 1-pound package frozen phyllo pastry sheets, thawed

Drain the chopped spinach very well by squeezing it between two plates. Set aside. Sauté the onions in a small amount of butter. Mix together the onions, eggs, scallions, feta cheese, dill, and parsley and add this mixture to the spinach. Season with salt, pepper, and nutmeg.

Brush the bottom of a 9-by-11-inch or 11-by-15-inch baking pan with melted butter. Cover the bottom of the pan with half the phyllo sheets, brushing each sheet with melted butter. Spread on the spinach mixture and top it with the remaining phyllo sheets. Be sure to brush each sheet with butter before putting on the next one.

Bake in a preheated 350° oven for about 1 hour or until the spanakopita is brown and puffy.

Wild Rice with Shiitake Mushrooms

THE OAKVILLE GROCERY COMPANY, SAN FRANCISCO

Serves 8 as a side dish, or stuffs six squab or a 14-pound turkey

If you can't find fresh shiitake mushrooms, reconstitute about ¼ pound of the dried ones in lukewarm water for about 20 minutes. (The dried ones are available in Oriental grocery stores.) Other mushrooms can, of course, be substituted, but it is the nutty flavor of the shiitake that makes this dish especially memorable.

1 cup wild rice
4 tablespoons minced shallots
6 tablespoons butter
8 large shiitake, stems removed and caps sliced

3 cups chicken stock or broth (but have more on hand as the dish may require longer cooking)
¼ cup minced parsley
Salt and freshly ground black pepper to taste

Bring 4 quarts of water to a boil. Add the wild rice and gently cook it for 15 minutes. Drain.

Sauté the shallots, just to the wilting point, in the butter. Add the shiitake and toss with the butter. Add the rice and toss. Add 1½ cups of chicken stock or broth and simmer the rice, covered, until the stock is absorbed. Continue with the remaining stock until the rice is tender, about 20 minutes. Add the parsley, salt, and pepper, and, as elegant options, 1 cup light cream or ½ cup mixed pine nuts and currants. Serve immediately.

Ratatouille

Serves 8 to 10

GRETCHEN'S OF COURSE, SEATTLE

This ratatouille profits from long, slow cooking in the oven, and also improves with overnight refrigeration.

½ cup olive oil
2 large onions, sliced
2 large cloves garlic, minced
2 teaspoons salt, or to taste
½ teaspoon freshly ground
    black pepper
1 teaspoon basil
1 teaspoon oregano

½ cup minced parsley
1 eggplant, cut into ½-inch
    cubes
6 zucchini, thickly sliced
2 green or red bell peppers,
    seeded and cut into chunks
4 large tomatoes, cut in
    wedges

In a large oven-proof casserole or Dutch oven, heat 2 tablespoons of the olive oil and sauté the onions and garlic. Mix together the salt, pepper, basil, oregano, and parsley. Layer the eggplant, zucchini, and peppers separately over the onions, sprinkling each layer with some of the herb mixture before adding the next vegetable. Drizzle the remaining oil over the top.

Cover the casserole and bake in a preheated 250° oven for 3 hours. Add the tomatoes. With a spatula, lightly turn the vegetables to mix. Continue to bake for another hour, or until the vegetables are tender. If the ratatouille is too soupy, bake it uncovered to allow the excess moisture to evaporate. Refrigerate overnight to blend the flavors.

White Bean and Caviar Salad   *Serves 10*

VIVANDE, SAN FRANCISCO

In the heart of the burgeoning upper Fillmore district of San Francisco, Carlo Middione opened Vivande, a delicatessen/ trattoria, in 1981. Formerly with the community relations office of the San Francisco Redevelopment Agency, he left that job to become a cooking school teacher. But that wasn't enough. Like his Sicilian father (who had had his own trattoria in southern California) before him, Carlo Middione wanted a trattoria. Now he has it — a long, narrow store filled with succulent olive oils and rare vinegars, crusty breads and pungent sausages, shallots and rice and beans, and cases of colorful salads, terrines, and galantines. Although much of his cooking is Sicilian, this salad is of Tuscan origin and is often served warm.

1 pound dried white beans, preferably cannellini
2 stalks celery, including the leaves
1 medium Bermuda onion, finely chopped
½ cup chopped parsley

3¾ ounces small black caviar
½ cup (generous) *salsa di limone* (see recipe below)
2 large lemons (for garnish)
Bermuda onion cut into thin rings (optional additional garnish)

Wash the beans and drain them. Put them in a heavy, deep, 4- or 5-quart pot. Cover them with 2 quarts of cold water and bring them to a *gentle* boil, covered. The boil must be gentle to keep the beans from breaking. Remove them from the heat and let them soak, still covered, for 1 hour. Drain them and return them to the pot with 2 quarts of fresh water. Add the celery and bring the pot to a slow simmer. Cook the beans gently for 20 minutes. Add the salt and cook the beans until tender but still slightly chewy. Discard the celery and drain the beans well. Put them in the refrigerator immediately to cool thoroughly.

Mix the cold beans with the onion, parsley, and caviar. Add the *salsa di limone* and toss the beans thoroughly. Place them in a serving bowl and decorate them with the lemon slices and, if you like, the Bermuda onion. This salad may be made a day ahead, but it should not be garnished until you are ready to serve it. With Melba toast or unsalted crackers, it makes a fine first course, or it can be part of a buffet supper.

Salsa di Limone

Whisk together three parts olive oil to one part fresh lemon juice, adding plenty of salt and black pepper. When the dressing is well emulsified, taste it. If it is too oily, add a little more salt, or add more lemon juice if it suits you.

Brussels Sprouts Salad

Serves 6 to 8

REBECCA'S, BOSTON

There simply *had* to be some way to make Brussels sprouts interesting, Rebecca Caras, who started the gourmet take-out trend in Boston in the late 1970s, decided. The sweet-and-sour dressing for this salad proved to be the answer.

2 pints Brussels sprouts
1 carrot, cut into ½-inch half moons
⅓ red onion, chopped

1 sweet red pepper, cut into julienne strips
2 strips cooked bacon, crumbled

Dressing

½ cup cider vinegar
¼ cup sugar
½ cup salad oil
¼ cup Burgundy

1¼ tablespoons red wine vinegar
Salt and freshly ground black pepper to taste

Boil or steam the Brussels sprouts until they are bright green and semifirm. Blanch the carrots. Make the dressing and combine it with all the salad ingredients. Serve chilled.

Rice Salad with Peanuts and Snow Peas

McMEAD'S, MIAMI, FLORIDA

Serves 6 to 8

Situated in the shadow of the exclusive shops known as Mayfair in Coconut Grove, Miami's oldest community, McMead's was an instant success when it opened in May 1981, and it has been ever since, filled as it is with palate-pleasing delicacies.

This white- and wild-rice salad that chef David Green prepares is one of them.

3 cups cooked white rice
1 cup cooked wild rice
½ cup snow peas, blanched
½ cup crushed salted peanuts
1 tablespoon sesame oil
1 tablespoon peanut oil

¼ cup olive oil
Salt and freshly ground black
  pepper to taste
Tabasco to taste
Chopped parsley to taste

Combine the two rices, the snow peas, and the peanuts. Toss them with the oils and season with the salt and pepper, Tabasco, and parsley.

Artichoke and Carrot Salad   *Serves 6 to 8*
PRIME CONCERN, GREAT NECK, LONG ISLAND

Delicious dishes need not be complicated, as this quick, simple salad created by Artie Nikolis for this popular Long Island take-out shop demonstrates. Key to Artie's success are her unusual combinations of ingredients.

1 16-ounce can artichoke
  hearts
2 onions, sliced
6 carrots, sliced
¼ cup oil

½ cup chopped parsley
Juice of 2 lemons
Salt and freshly ground black
  pepper to taste

Drain the artichokes and cut them in half. Sauté the onions and carrots in the oil until they are just soft. Add the artichokes and heat thoroughly. Add the parsley and lemon juice. Season with salt and pepper. Serve hot or cold.

Zucchini Mufaletta Salad

Serves 8

POULET, BERKELEY

Straightforward, honest, hearty country flavors, including garlic, are among the trademarks of chef Bruce Aidell's cuisine at Poulet. He is, in fact, food editor of the newsletter for the nationwide Garlic Club, which has a membership of some two thousand garlic aficionados. It comes as no surprise, then, that four cloves of garlic flavor the dressing in this zucchini salad.

Olive Dressing

1½ cups pitted Calamata olives, chopped

1 cup pitted Italian green olives, chopped

½ cup olive oil

½ cup chopped parsley

⅓ cup chopped pimientos

4 anchovy fillets, finely chopped

2 tablespoons capers

1 teaspoon oregano

4 cloves garlic, finely chopped

½ red onion, finely chopped

½ cup pesto sauce, such as the one on page 176 (optional)

Freshly ground black pepper

½ cup red wine vinegar

Salad

3 pounds zucchini, cut into 2-by-½-inch spears

½ pound carrots, cut into 2-by-½-inch spears

½ pound Swiss cheese, cut into ¼-inch-thick julienne strips

Combine all the ingredients for the olive dressing and let them sit, refrigerated, for 2 hours or overnight. (This dressing will keep for more than a week.)

To make the salad, blanch the zucchini for 45 seconds in boiling water and refresh it under cold water. Blanch the carrots for 6 minutes and refresh them under cold water. Combine the vegetables, cheese, and olive dressing. Chill and serve.

Broccoli-Mushroom Salad

Serves 6

FORMAGGIO KITCHEN, CAMBRIDGE

This was a spur-of-the-moment invention, made for a Woman's Culinary Guild luncheon at Julia Child's home. It was a great success, judging from the number of requests for the recipe that Formaggio's received from the women who attended the lunch. The dressing is the same one the shop normally uses on its potato salad.

1 bunch parsley
Juice of 4 lemons
7 anchovy fillets
Freshly ground black pepper
   to taste

1 cup olive oil
1 pound broccoli flowerets,
   blanched
½ pound mushrooms, thinly
   sliced

Put the parsley leaves, lemon juice, anchovies, and pepper into the bowl of a food processor. Blend, and then slowly add the oil until the mixture thickens. Pour the dressing over the broccoli and mushrooms and toss gently.

159

Broccoli with Lemon and Olive Oil   *Serves 6*

WASHINGTON MARKET, NEW YORK CITY (TRIBECA)

A very easy dish and one that proves that simple food is often the best. When chef Jaclyn Veneroso makes this, she uses extra-virgin olive oil, but obviously you can use the one you have on hand.

2 small heads of broccoli
Juice of 2 lemons

Salt and freshly ground black
pepper to taste
¼ cup extra-virgin olive oil

Trim the broccoli, separating the flowerets from the stems. (Do not use the stems in this dish.) Steam the flowerets until they are tender but still bright green. Remove them from the steamer immediately so that they don't overcook.

Put the lemon juice and salt and pepper in a medium-sized bowl. While beating with a wire whisk, gradually add the olive oil.

While the broccoli is still warm, toss it with the dressing. Serve cold.

Sweet-Sour Cucumber Salad   *Serves 6*

THE MARKET OF THE COMMISSARY, PHILADELPHIA

At The Market, this dish is always on hand. The chefs recommend it as an accompaniment for curry entrées, including the lamb curry with eggplant on page 103.

2 medium cucumbers, cut in
half lengthwise and thinly
sliced
¼ cup white vinegar

1 tablespoon sugar
½ teaspoon salt
½ teaspoon freshly ground
black pepper

160

Combine all the ingredients and let the cucumbers marinate for several hours in the refrigerator. If you like, sprinkle with chopped roasted peanuts before serving.

Celeriac Rémoulade *Serves 6*

NEUMAN & BOGDONOFF, NEW YORK CITY
 (UPPER EAST SIDE)

With its combination of Pommery and Dijon mustards, this makes a hearty midwinter salad and an excellent accompaniment to pâté. Celeriac (sometimes called knob celery or celery root) has all the good taste of celery without the stringy, watery consistency.

2 to 3 celeriacs (about 3
  pounds)
2 cups mayonnaise
¾ cup Dijon mustard
½ cup Pommery mustard

Dash of Tabasco
Juice of 1 lemon
Salt and freshly ground black
  pepper to taste

Trim and peel the celeriacs and drop them into cold water with a little lemon juice to prevent them from turning brown.

Combine the remaining ingredients.

Remove the celery roots from the water, one at a time, and cut in half. Scoop out the spongy center and cut the rest into julienne strips. Immediately stir the strips into the dressing. Continue until all the celeriac has been used. Chill. Serve cold.

Potato Salad without Mayonnaise   Serves 6 to 8

THE AMERICAN CAFÉ MARKET, WASHINGTON, D.C.

"What makes the American Café unique," said James Beard, "is that it has the sort of food people love to eat and seldom find well prepared." This potato salad is a good example.

2 pounds red or brown new potatoes, unpeeled

3 eggs

2 tablespoons plus 1 teaspoon salt

½ cup white wine

1 tablespoon wine vinegar

1 tablespoon Dijon mustard

2 tablespoons chopped dill weed

½ teaspoon freshly ground black pepper

1 teaspoon thyme

½ cup olive oil

1 small red onion, sliced into rings

6 green Spanish olives, sliced (optional)

Put the potatoes, eggs, and 2 tablespoons of salt into a pot of warm water. Bring the water to a boil and simmer for 8 minutes. Remove the eggs and put them in the refrigerator (chilling them facilitates peeling). Continue cooking the potatoes until they are just tender. Drain the potatoes and put them in a bowl of cold water.

Put the wine, vinegar, mustard, dill, 1 teaspoon salt, and pepper into a large bowl and mix with a whisk. Whisk in the olive oil slowly until the dressing is smooth.

When the potatoes are cool enough to handle, cut them into ⅜-inch slices and stir them into the dressing. Peel and slice the eggs, and add them to the salad. Add the onions and olives and mix everything together. Refrigerate the salad until an hour or so before serving. Serve at room temperature.

162

German-Style Potato Salad

ZABAR'S, NEW YORK CITY (UPPER WEST SIDE)

Old-fashioned German potato salad, in which bacon fat substitutes for mayonnaise, is ever popular at Zabar's take-out counter. Although it is traditionally served warm, it is good cold, too.

6 slices bacon
2 tablespoons reserved
  drippings
2 tablespoons sugar
1 teaspoon all-purpose flour
Salt and freshly ground black
  pepper to taste

¼ cup red wine vinegar
½ cup water
1 large onion, finely chopped
2 pounds potatoes, cooked,
  peeled, and sliced
1 tablespoon chopped fresh
  dill (optional)

Sauté the bacon until it is crisp. Drain and crumble it. In the pan with the reserved bacon drippings, mix the sugar, flour, salt, and pepper until smooth. Stir in the vinegar and water and bring the mixture to a boil. Add the onion and mix well. Add the potato slices, stirring gently to make sure that they are coated with dressing. Transfer the salad to a bowl and serve it topped with the crumbled bacon and chopped dill.

Vegetable Salad in Creamy Vinaigrette

THE WATERGATE CHEFS, WASHINGTON, D.C.   *Serves 6 to 8*

The Watergate Chefs is the name of the gourmet food shop in the Watergate hotel-apartment-office complex, but it also stands for four chefs, each of whom contributes his specialties. This dish, by Richard Sultani, is the most popular salad.

The vinaigrette recipe makes about a quart of dressing, more than you need for this salad. But it keeps well in a tightly covered jar in the refrigerator and is excellent on a tossed green salad. (You can halve the recipe by beating the egg yolk and then dividing it in half.)

½ head cauliflower
4 stalks celery
2 green peppers
4 carrots

¾ pound green beans
Creamy vinaigrette (see recipe below)

Wash, trim, and cut the cauliflower, celery, and green peppers into bite-size pieces.

Cut the carrots and green beans into bite-size pieces and blanch them in boiling water for 1 to 2 minutes. Cool them in ice water, and drain.

Put all the vegetables into a bowl and add enough dressing to coat them. Toss well. Serve cold.

Creamy Vinaigrette

1 egg yolk
2 tablespoons Dijon mustard
½ cup red wine vinegar
3 to 4 cups salad or olive oil
2 tablespoons chopped shallots

1 tablespoon chopped tarragon
2 tablespoons chopped parsley
Salt and freshly ground black pepper to taste

Combine the egg yolk, mustard, and vinegar with a wire whisk. Slowly add the oil, while continuing to whisk, until the dressing becomes thick and creamy. Add the chopped herbs and the salt and pepper. Store the dressing in the refrigerator.

Piper's Potpourri *Serves 8*

THE FRUIT LADY, PHILADELPHIA

Although Joan Arensberg and Phyllis Brodsky (who together are The Fruit Lady) have catered parties for Pennsylvania's governor and other VIPs, they take just as much interest in the food they serve the office workers around them. Witness this nutritious sprout salad.

½ pound bean sprouts
1 head broccoli flowerets, blanched
2 red peppers, cut in strips
1 1-pound can tiny corn kernels

2 cloves garlic
3 tablespoons Dijon mustard
¾ cup red wine vinegar
1¼ cups oil
Salt and freshly ground black pepper to taste

Place the first four ingredients in a large bowl and stir gently.

To make the vinaigrette, put the garlic, mustard, and vinegar in a blender or food processor and blend, adding the oil slowly. Add the salt and pepper. Toss the dressing with the salad.

Mexican Pineapple-Cabbage Salad   *Serves 6 to 8*
JIM JAMAIL & SONS FOOD MARKET, HOUSTON

In fast-paced space-age Houston, Jamail's is something of an anachronism, with its emphasis on quality and service and its long tradition. Negeeb Jamail, father of the present owner, came to Houston from Lebanon in 1905. From open-air vendor of produce, he rose to become the owner of one of Houston's finest stores. Today's market is still very much a family affair, as Negeeb's three sons and their children work there.

Even the take-out department of Jamail's has stood the test of time. Chef Rolf Mietler joined the staff in 1968, long before gourmet take-out became all the rage. You'll find more of his creations in the Salads chapter.

½ large white cabbage
2 medium carrots, scraped
1½ cups canned crushed
  pineapple, drained
1 cup mayonnaise

Juice of 2 limes
1 teaspoon celery salt
Salt and freshly ground black
  pepper to taste

Shred the cabbage and the carrots very fine. Put them in a bowl with the drained pineapple. Mix together the mayonnaise, lime juice, and celery salt and add to the bowl. Stir well and season with salt and pepper. Serve cold.

Pear and Endive Salad   *Serves 4*
THE SILVER PALATE, NEW YORK CITY (UPPER WEST SIDE)

Cozy is the word customers use to describe their favorite West Side gourmet take-out shop. In spite of its success, The Silver

166

Palate has remained in the 11-by-16-foot store where it all began in 1977. But the kitchen has been set up around the corner in a brownstone, and their packaged products are put up in small batches in a nearby cannery. The tiny size hasn't hurt the shop, according to its owners, Sheila Lukins and Julee Rosso, because a crammed store creates a sense of excitement. Of course, the reason people cram into it is the exquisite food that has made The Silver Palate famous.

The walnut oil called for in this recipe can be purchased from the shop — or from almost any specialty food store.

2 heads Belgian endive
2 ripe pears, preferably Anjou
6 ounces crumbly Gorgonzola
  cheese
¼ cup coarsely chopped
  walnuts
White wine vinaigrette (see
  recipe below)

Break the leaves of the endive off at the base and wash and dry them thoroughly. Arrange four or five leaves on each of four salad plates.

Quarter and core the unpeeled pears. Slice each quarter into five pieces. Arrange the pear slices over the endive in a fan design. Crumble the Gorgonzola over each plate and then sprinkle the nuts over all. Whisk the vinaigrette and drizzle it over the salad.

White Wine Vinaigrette

½ cup white wine vinegar
¼ teaspoon freshly ground
  black pepper
⅛ teaspoon ground fennel
Pinch of salt
Pinch of sugar
1 cup walnut oil

Pour the vinegar into a small mixing bowl. Add the pepper, fennel, salt, and sugar. Gradually add the oil, whisking constantly. This recipe makes 1½ cups of dressing.

Sugar Snap Peas and Raspberries   *Serves 4 to 6*
THE BLACK FOREST, CAMBRIDGE

Separately, there are few foods to compare with sugar snap peas or raspberries; together they are a delectable combination. Fortunately, they come into their all-too-brief seasons at the same time, but if you can't find raspberries, you could substitute blueberries. Raspberry vinegar is available in gourmet food shops.

1 pound sugar snap peas
Pinch of salt
½ pint fresh raspberries

6 tablespoons olive oil
2 tablespoons raspberry vinegar

Trim the ends off the peas and toss them, uncooked, with a pinch of salt. Wash the berries and add them to the peas. Combine the oil and vinegar and stir it very gently through the peas and berries so as not to break the berries. Serve chilled.

Gingered Pear Salad   *Serves 8 to 10*
THE GOURMET GROCER, PRAIRIE VILLAGE, KANSAS

Tom Anderson is a native Kansan who quit Kansas City a few years ago for Washington State. There he put his culinary skills to use in a French restaurant in Spokane, but he tired of the late nights in restaurant life and longed to be back home in Kansas; so last year he returned and opened one of Kansas City's first gourmet take-out shops, in suburban Prairie Village. He emphasizes that fresh ginger is essential in this recipe.

6 ripe Bartlett pears, peeled
6 Jonathan or Delicious apples
½ pound white seedless grapes
2 stalks celery
1 cup mayonnaise

1 tablespoon milk
1 tablespoon lemon juice
1 tablespoon freshly grated
  gingerroot
1 cup pecans

Cut up the fruits and chop the celery and toss them lightly with the mayonnaise, milk, lemon juice, and gingerroot. Add the pecans and again toss lightly. This is a very rich salad, so servings should be small.

Honey-Glazed Carrot Salad   *Serves 4*

McMEAD'S, MIAMI, FLORIDA

Prime meats, fresh produce, select wines and beers, and a high-ceilinged New York—loft look all help to make McMead's a popular spot in Coconut Grove. The movie moguls who have recently become a part of the scene in this historic section of Miami are among its most devoted clientele. Honey-glazed carrot salad, of course, is easy on any waistline.

6 cups coarsely grated carrots
1 cup Dijon mustard
½ cup honey
1 teaspoon ground ginger

Juice of 1 lemon
Salt and freshly ground white
  pepper to taste

Combine the carrots with the other ingredients, chill thoroughly, and serve.

169

Persimmon Salad

THE OAKVILLE GROCERY COMPANY, SAN FRANCISCO

Clark Wolf, the young manager of San Francisco's Oakville Grocery, traveled to Berlin, Paris, Milan, Munich, and London studying epicurean food shops to ready himself for his job as a gourmet marketeer. Now there's scarcely a fruit or vegetable, cheese or sausage he can't identify. The Fu Yo persimmons in this salad are a case in point. They are popular California persimmons that are sweet and edible while they are still firm. If they can't be had, Bosc pears make a good substitute, according to Rick O'Connell, food specialist at the grocery and creator of this recipe.

6 Fu Yo persimmons
1 bunch watercress
3 Belgian endives
1 cup shelled pecans, sautéed in a little light olive oil to bring out the flavor

Raspberry, blueberry, or sherry vinegar
Olive oil
Salt and freshly ground black pepper to taste

Do not peel the persimmons, but slice them about ¼ inch thick. Cut the endive lengthwise down the center, then diagonally in 1-inch pieces. Toss gently with the persimmon slices. Scatter the watercress leaves on top and then the pecans. Prepare about ¾ cup of dressing, using half oil and half vinegar with blueberry or raspberry vinegar, or 1 part vinegar to 3 parts oil with sherry vinegar. Season the dressing with salt and pepper and pour it over the salad just before serving.

Note: If you substitute pears for the persimmons, quarter but do not peel them, and slice them about ¼ inch thick.

Sauces

Winter Tomato Sauce

Makes about 5 cups

PASTA, INC., WASHINGTON, D.C.

Nadine Kalachnikoff, the daughter of a Russian émigré father and a Spanish mother, grew up traveling extensively and learning to like the foods of all nations. She also learned how to cook many of them, because she and her three sisters had three chores to choose from: cooking, washing dishes, or setting the table. Cooking was, in Nadine's estimation, by far the most desirable of the three. So it followed that she decided to make her living in gourmet foods. Georgetown's Pasta, Inc., was the capital's first fresh pasta shop, and this tomato sauce is one of Nadine's most popular toppings. Recipes for two of her other sauces appear later.

1 onion, finely ground
2 tablespoons plus 1 teaspoon olive oil
5 teaspoons butter
About 5 large cloves garlic, 1 whole and 4 chopped
½ cup dry red wine
2 cans (29 ounces each) tomatoes

10 ounces tomato purée
½ bay leaf
1½ teaspoons dried basil
1 teaspoon sugar
1 tablespoon plus 1 teaspoon oregano leaves
Salt and freshly ground black pepper to taste

Sauté the onion in the oil and butter until it is translucent. Add a whole clove of peeled garlic and sauté it for about 1 minute. Remove the garlic clove. Add the wine and stir the mixture well. Crush the tomatoes with your hands, leaving them lumpy, and add them to the pan, along with the purée. Bring the sauce to a boil. Reduce the heat to low. Add the remaining ingredients and simmer, uncovered, for about 1½ hours, stirring occasionally.

172

Mushroom Vinaigrette

Makes about 3 cups

OUISIE'S TABLE AND THE TRAVELING
BROWN BAG LUNCH CO., HOUSTON

Elouise Cooper doesn't mind seeing her cold dishes leave the shop, but she really would prefer that people sat down and ate hot meals in the restaurant, where she could be sure they were getting the food the way it was intended to be served. Still, her customers insist on taking home whole meals — including a medium-rare beef tenderloin stuffed with lump crab meat, which makes her very nervous — and they keep coming back for more.

This sauce doesn't present any such problems. It is designed to be served over a sliced cold sirloin of beef, an elegant buffet platter, and it would certainly elevate any leftover steak or roast to new heights.

½ cup fresh lemon juice
¼ cup red wine
½ teaspoon thyme
1 teaspoon basil
1 teaspoon chervil
1 tablespoon Tabasco
1 teaspoon Dijon mustard
2 large cloves garlic, minced
1½ cups light olive oil

Salt to taste
1 pound fresh mushrooms, thinly sliced
½ bunch green onions, finely chopped
12 to 18 cherry tomatoes, cut in half
A handful of chopped parsley

Whisk together the lemon juice, wine, herbs, Tabasco, mustard, and garlic. Drizzle in the olive oil, whisking steadily. Taste for salt, and add some if necessary.

Just before you are ready to use the sauce, pour it over the mushrooms, onions, tomatoes, and parsley, and mix all together.

Mushroom Sauce à la Veronese

Serves 4 to 6

PASTA, INC., WASHINGTON, D.C.

Nadine Kalachnikoff would one day like to expand her Pasta, Inc., to include a string of subsidiaries in the suburbs. This sauce, one of her specialties, is excellent not only for pasta but for chicken, steak, veal, or Veronese risotto.

1 teaspoon butter
1 tablespoon olive oil
1 small onion, chopped
Handful of chopped parsley
1 clove garlic, chopped

1 to 2 tablespoons flour
½ pound mushrooms, sliced
Salt and freshly ground black
 pepper to taste
Dollop of butter

In the butter and olive oil, sauté the onion, parsley, and garlic until the onion is transparent. Then sprinkle the mixture with the flour, add the mushrooms and salt and pepper, and simmer the sauce until the mushrooms are cooked. The liquid that comes from the mushrooms should be sufficient to make a slightly thickened sauce. Before serving it, add a dollop of butter.

Walnut Sauce

Makes 3 cups

THE FRUIT LADY, PHILADELPHIA

Thick with walnuts and lightly touched with garlic, this sauce makes pasta quite exotic.

2 cups walnuts
½ cup heavy cream
½ cup lukewarm water
2 cloves garlic

1 tablespoon marjoram
4 tablespoons melted butter
2 teaspoons salt

174

Blend all the ingredients in a food processor. The sauce will be very thick and may need to be thinned with light cream, and the seasonings may need to be adjusted.

To serve, cook any pasta as directed. Drain it and return it to a heavy saucepan. Combine it with the walnut sauce and toss briefly over a low flame.

Shrimp and Feta Pasta Sauce   *Serves 6 to 8*

GOODIES TO GO, LEXINGTON, MASSACHUSETTS

Although this tangy sauce is meant to go over pasta, it's equally good served as a topping for a bed of rice. Either way, it's a good idea to liberally sprinkle additional crumbled feta on the base before adding the sauce.

3 or 4 cloves garlic, minced
¼ to ½ cup olive oil
2 12-ounce cans stewed
  tomatoes
2 tablespoons parsley, chopped
1 tablespoon oregano

Salt and pepper to taste
1 can pitted black olives
  (optional)
Dash of red wine (optional)
1 pound raw shrimp
⅓ pound feta cheese, crumbled

Sauté the garlic in the olive oil until lightly browned. Add the stewed tomatoes, parsley, oregano, salt, and pepper (and the olives and wine if you wish to use them), and let the sauce simmer until thick.

Meanwhile, peel and devein the shrimp. Cook it in boiling water for 3 to 4 minutes, drain it, and set it aside.

Add the feta to the sauce and simmer for 30 minutes or so. Add the shrimp and cook for another 5 minutes.

Marinara Sauce

FETTUCCINE BROS., SAN FRANCISCO

If the name of your shop is Fettuccine Bros. and you specialize in pasta, you are also likely to specialize in sauces. This basic marinara can be varied according to the suggestions below or to your own taste.

1 large onion, chopped
½ cup butter
1 bay leaf
3 or 4 cloves garlic, chopped

2 28-ounce cans imported plum tomatoes, drained and chopped
2 teaspoons oregano
Salt and freshly ground black pepper to taste

Sauté the onion in the butter until it is almost wilted. Add the bay leaf and garlic and continue to sauté for 1 minute. Add the tomatoes, oregano, and pepper and simmer for 20 minutes. Season to taste with salt.

Note: If you wish, sauté 2 cups of chopped pancetta or prosciutto along with the onions. Pour off the fat and add the meat to the sauce. Or you might add 2 cups of thinly sliced fresh vegetables during the last 5 minutes of cooking.

Pesto

Serves 4

CAVIAR ETCETERA, WOODBURY, LONG ISLAND

When your garden or the local farmers' market is awash in basil, you can make up many batches of this recipe and freeze them for winter use.

1 cup olive oil	1 tablespoon pine nuts
¼ cup chopped garlic	1 tablespoon heavy cream
1 bunch fresh basil, well washed and dried	1 ounce cream cheese, Italian or regular

Using a blender or food processor, blend half the oil with all the other ingredients. When the mixture is smooth, blend in the remaining oil slowly.

Tomato-Olive Pasta Sauce (Sauce Savoia)

GOURMET PASTA, GREAT NECK, LONG ISLAND,   *Serves 4*
    AND NEW YORK CITY (UPPER EAST SIDE)

This pasta sauce is one of the quickest you can make, especially if you use a food processor to mince the onions, tomatoes, and olives and chop the herbs. It always meets with raves and requests for more. If fresh herbs are not available, use half the quantity of dried.

1 small onion, minced	2 tablespoons chopped fresh thyme
2 tablespoons olive oil	
5 large ripe tomatoes, minced	1 tablespoon freshly ground black pepper
2 tablespoons chopped fresh oregano	1 cup pitted black olives, minced
2 tablespoons chopped fresh sage	4 tablespoons freshly grated Parmesan cheese
2 tablespoons chopped fresh basil	

Sauté the onion in the olive oil until soft. Add the tomatoes, herbs, and pepper. Simmer for 5 minutes. Add the olives and cheese. Simmer 5 minutes longer.

Toss the cooked pasta of your choice with the sauce and serve with additional grated Parmesan and freshly ground black pepper.

Shrimp Sauce

PASTA, INC., WASHINGTON, D.C.

Rice, eggs, fish, and spaghetti are all good bases for this shrimp sauce.

1 tablespoon pine nuts
2 small onions, chopped
2 tablespoons soya oil
2 tablespoons butter

1½ tablespoons chopped parsley
12 raw shrimp, shelled and cut up
3 or 4 tablespoons warm water

Roast the pine nuts in a frying pan for a few minutes. Crush them, using a mortar and pestle. Set them aside.

Sauté the chopped onions in the oil and butter until limp and transparent. Add the parsley, shrimp, and pine nuts and stir. Add the warm water and simmer the sauce very slowly for 4 to 5 minutes until the shrimp are just cooked. This sauce may be served as it is or put through a sieve.

Spicy Mustard

Makes approximately 1½ cups

SI BON, SANIBEL, FLORIDA

This sauce is excellent with ham or corned beef.

½ cup Colman's dry mustard
½ cup sugar
½ cup white vinegar

1 egg, beaten
1 cup heavy cream, whipped

Combine the mustard, sugar, and vinegar and let the mixture stand overnight. The next day, put it in the top of a double boiler and add the beaten egg. Cook it until it is thick, stirring constantly. When it is cool, fold in the whipped cream.

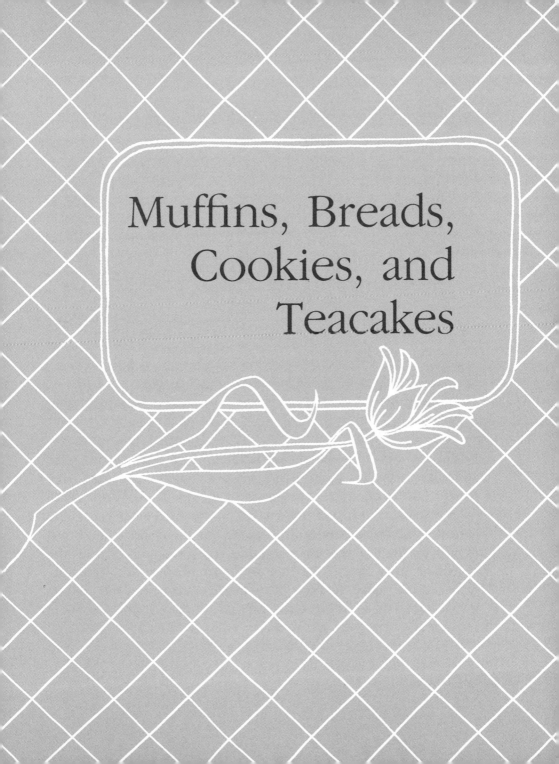

Muffins, Breads, Cookies, and Teacakes

Galettes au Fromage

Makes about 30 wafers

A LA CARTE AT GILLIEWRINKLES,
    COLD SPRING HARBOR, LONG ISLAND

Katharine Irwin sells her A la Carte foods from her home, but when a group of women in Cold Spring Harbor opened a boutique to market handmade crafts a few years ago, they asked her if she would put a few of her culinary creations in their shop. Called Gilliewrinkles, it is one of the most attractive stores in this quaint North Shore town. Its glass-doored freezer is filled with Irwin specialties like these lacy cheese wafers — they're good as a savory after the meal, or with drinks.

½ pound imported Swiss cheese, grated
½ cup imported Parmesan cheese, grated
½ pound butter, at room temperature

¾ cup sifted all-purpose flour (be sure to sift before measuring)
⅛ teaspoon cayenne
¼ teaspoon salt
1 egg beaten with 1 teaspoon water

Knead 1½ cups of Swiss cheese with the Parmesan, butter, flour, and spices. Form the mixture into a ball and chill. Preheat the oven to 425°. Break off scant tablespoons of the dough, form them into balls, and flatten into very thin circles on a greased baking sheet. Be sure to leave space between the wafers for some spreading. Brush them with the egg and water mixture and sprinkle them with the remaining Swiss cheese. Bake for about 10 minutes, or until lightly browned and puffed. Remove the wafers from the oven and cool on a cake rack. These freeze well and can be served either at room temperature or slightly warmed.

Mexican Braided Bread with Brie   *Serves 25*

CAMPBELL AND CO.'S "A MATTER OF TASTE,"
BOCA RATON, FLORIDA

Faun Campbell and her son, Gregory, were so much in demand as caterers for Boca Raton parties that they started freez-
ing their hors d'oeuvres so there would always be something
available for emergencies. Three years ago they opened a gourmet take-out shop featuring freezers filled with hors d'oeuvres
and pastries. This is one of their most handsome creations. (Directions for a half-size braided bread with Camembert are at
the end of the recipe.)

2 cups water	2 tablespoons active dry yeast
1½ tablespoons sugar	6 cups all-purpose flour
1 tablespoon salt	1-kilo wheel of Brie
2 tablespoons butter	

Combine the water, sugar, salt, and butter in a saucepan and heat to
between 110° and 115° (just slightly warmer than lukewarm). Pour
this mixture into a warmed bowl and add the yeast. Cover the bowl
and let the mixture stand until bubbly.

Sift in the flour gradually. Knead until the dough is velvet
smooth and does not stick to your hands. Place it in a greased bowl,
set the bowl in a warm place, and let the dough rise until double in
bulk.

Punch the dough down and divide it into three pieces. Roll
each piece into a long rope on a floured surface. Braid the strands
together and form the dough around a greased 8-inch round cake
tin laid on a greased cookie sheet. Make a bow with the leftover
dough and use it to fasten the end of the braid. Cover and let the
dough rise for about 30 minutes.

Preheat oven to 375°.

Make a wash of beaten egg and water and brush it on the braid. Bake for 20 minutes. Brush it again with the egg wash; return it to the oven and continue baking for another 15 to 20 minutes. (Check the bottom from time to time to make sure the bread is not burning.) Put it on a rack to cool. Place a 1-kilo wheel of Brie in the center of the braid and serve on a round cheese board.

For a smaller number of guests, halve the recipe. Mold the dough around an empty Camembert box, about 5 inches in diameter, greased and wrapped in aluminum foil. Grease the outside of the foil as well before knotting the dough around it. Bake as for the larger braid, but reduce the baking time by 5 to 10 minutes. Serve with the Camembert in the center.

Cheddar Cheese Muffins   *Makes about 2 dozen*

E.A.T., NEW YORK CITY (UPPER EAST SIDE)

These tangy muffins created by Eli Zabar have an unusual texture. When you are making them, if the dough seems soft, don't despair — all works out in the end.

2 cups milk
2 tablespoons active dry yeast
12 tablespoons (1½ sticks) unsalted butter

6 ounces Cheddar cheese, crumbled
6 cups all-purpose flour

Scald the milk and cool it to lukewarm. Dissolve the yeast in 1 cup of it. Then add the second cup of milk. Set the milk-yeast mixture aside.

Put the cheese, butter, and flour in the bowl of an electric

182

mixer and mix on low speed until crumbly and pea-sized. Add the milk-yeast mixture and mix for 1 or 2 minutes until the batter is evenly moist. Pour the batter into buttered muffin tins and let rise in a warm place until doubled in bulk. Bake in a preheated 375° oven for 12 to 15 minutes, or until done.

Scottish Shortbread

Makes 8 large wedges
or 16 small ones

THE CHARCUTERIE,
WELLESLEY, MASSACHUSETTS

This easy recipe produces a marvelously silky shortbread. The addition of rice flour, according to Charcuterie co-owner John Gordon, makes it authentic.

1 cup (2 sticks) unsalted
   butter
½ cup sugar
2 cups all-purpose flour

1 cup rice flour
¼ teaspoon salt
1 egg white
1 teaspoon sugar

Cream together the butter and sugar. Combine the two flours with the salt and add slowly to the butter-and-sugar mixture until the dry ingredients are completely incorporated. The dough will be very dry and granular.

Press the dough into a greased 9-inch round pie plate. Crimp the edges with a fork and score the dough into eight or sixteen equal wedges. Brush with slightly beaten egg white and sprinkle with 1 teaspoon of sugar.

Bake in a preheated 325° oven for 35 minutes. While the shortbread is still warm, cut through the wedges to separate them. To serve, reassemble the cooled shortbread on a serving dish.

Fudge Squares

Makes about 40 1½-inch squares

CAMPBELL AND CO.'S "A MATTER OF TASTE,"
BOCA RATON, FLORIDA

If *your* taste runs to rich chocolate with a butter-cream frosting, these fudge squares will surely satisfy your sweet tooth.

1 cup shortening	1 cup all-purpose flour
4 tablespoons cocoa	½ teaspoon salt
4 eggs	1 tablespoon vanilla extract
2 cups sugar	1 cup chopped walnuts

Melt the shortening and add the cocoa. Stir together until well combined. Beat the eggs and sugar together until light, and then combine them with the cooled chocolate mixture.

Sift together the flour and salt and add to the chocolate mixture. Stir in the vanilla and chopped nuts. Pour the batter into a greased and floured 9-by-13-inch pan. Bake in a preheated 350° oven for 25 minutes. When cool, frost with the butter-cream frosting.

Butter-Cream Frosting

¾ cup butter	6 tablespoons milk
10 tablespoons cocoa	2 teaspoons vanilla extract
3 cups confectioner's sugar	

Cream together the butter, cocoa, and half the sugar. When thoroughly creamed, add the remainder of the sugar alternately with the milk and vanilla. Beat until the frosting is very creamy and of spreading consistency.

184

Amaretti (Almond Cookies)

VIVANDE, SAN FRANCISCO   *Makes 24 medium-sized cookies*

The sweets at Vivande are ever popular, whether they are tortes, cheese cakes, fruit desserts, or cookies. Carlo Middione's *amaretti* may be stored successfully in a tin or jar for two weeks or more.

2½ cups finely ground almonds
¼ cup granulated sugar

2 egg whites from "jumbo" eggs

Combine the almonds and sugar. Add the egg whites a little at a time until a firm but pliable paste has been formed. If it seems too soft, add more sugar and nuts. If it is too firm, add a *little* more egg white.

Butter and lightly flour a cookie sheet or line the cookie sheet with parchment paper. Spoon the dough onto it in rather large, flat button shapes. Leave plenty of space between them. Sprinkle a little granulated sugar on top of each. (If the dough seems a little too stiff despite the addition of egg white, let the cookies, sprinkled with sugar, stand for an hour or more before baking. This will help them to "relax" into a smooth shape. Many Italian cooks insist that this step is absolutely essential for good *amaretti.*) Bake the cookies in a preheated 350° oven for 15 minutes, or until they are golden brown. Beware, however, of over-browning them, for they burn easily.

Granny's Goodies

Makes 3 to 4 dozen cookies

GOODIES TO GO, LEXINGTON, MASSACHUSETTS

These easy-to-make, crisp and nutty oatmeal cookies will disappear from the cookie crock almost as fast as they're made. For variations on the plain oatmeal cookie theme, Gaye Pickrel sometimes adds nuts or dates, raisins or coconut — or a little of each — and says of them proudly, "They're terrific!"

1 cup white sugar	1 teaspoon baking soda
1 cup dark brown sugar	1 teaspoon baking powder
2 cups oatmeal	2 eggs
2 cups all-purpose flour	1 cup butter, melted
½ teaspoon salt	1 teaspoon vanilla extract

Combine the sugars, oatmeal, and flour sifted with the salt, baking soda, and baking powder. Beat the eggs and add them to the dry ingredients. Add the melted butter and mix thoroughly. Add the vanilla.

Roll the dough into 1-inch balls and place them on ungreased cookie sheets. Bake in a preheated 350° oven.

Orange Chocolate Teacake

FORMAGGIO KITCHEN, CAMBRIDGE

Serves 10 to 12

This is similar to the cake that follows, except that orange and chocolate substitute for the lemon and poppy seed.

1½ cups (3 sticks) unsalted butter, softened

1½ cups granulated sugar

2 oranges

1½ teaspoons Grand Marnier

8 eggs, separated, at room temperature

2 cups sifted cake flour

½ teaspoon salt

5 ounces semisweet chocolate, coarsely grated

Cream the butter in a large bowl. Gradually beat in all but ¼ cup of the sugar.

Grate the oranges. Squeeze them, and add enough orange juice to the zest to make ⅓ cup. Beat the orange juice and the Grand Marnier into the butter mixture. Add the egg yolks one at a time, beating thoroughly after each addition. Beat until the mixture is *very* light.

In a separate bowl, beat the egg whites until they form soft peaks. Add the remaining ¼ cup of sugar and beat until the whites are stiff but not dry.

Sift the flour and salt, one third at a time, over the egg yolk mixture, folding it in after each addition. Stir in a quarter of the egg whites and then fold in the remaining whites. Fold in the grated chocolate.

Pour the batter into a greased and floured 10-inch bundt pan. Bake in a preheated 350° oven for about 1 hour, until a toothpick inserted in the center of the cake comes out clean. Let cool for 5 minutes before turning the cake out onto a wire rack.

187

Lemon Poppy-Seed Teacake

Serves 10 to 12

FORMAGGIO KITCHEN, CAMBRIDGE

There are some people — many — who think this is the best teacake ever. Adrienne Houspian, who created it, has since moved to New York, first to Dean & DeLuca and more recently to Bloomingdale's, but Formaggio Kitchen's patrons still enjoy her marvelous desserts, this one in particular.

1½ cups (3 sticks) unsalted butter, softened
1½ cups granulated sugar
2 tablespoons grated lemon zest
1 tablespoon grated orange zest (or dried orange peel)

½ cup poppy seeds
8 eggs, separated, at room temperature
2 cups sifted cake flour
½ teaspoon salt
½ cup lemon juice
¼ to ⅓ cup superfine sugar

Cream the butter in a large bowl. Gradually beat in all but ¼ cup of the granulated sugar. Beat in the lemon and orange zests and the poppy seeds. Add the egg yolks one at a time, beating thoroughly after each addition. Beat until the mixture is very light.

In a separate bowl, beat the egg whites until they form soft peaks. Add the remaining ¼ cup of granulated sugar and beat until the whites are stiff but not dry.

Sift the flour and salt, one third at a time, over the egg yolk mixture, folding it in after each addition. Stir in a quarter of the egg whites and then fold in the remaining whites.

Pour the batter into a greased and floured 10-inch bundt pan. Bake in a preheated 350° oven for about 1 hour, until a toothpick inserted in the center of the cake comes out clean.

188

Cool the cake in the pan for 5 minutes. Unmold it over a wire rack and place the rack over a large bowl. Put the lemon juice into a measuring cup with a spout or a pitcher and stir in the superfine sugar until it is dissolved. Pour this mixture over the cake until the outside is moist all over but not soggy.

Cool the cake completely.

Rugelach
Serves 6 to 8

McMEAD'S, MIAMI, FLORIDA

This pastry — rich in coconut, walnuts, and raisins and slathered with apricot jam — isn't the sort of confection one eats every day, but every once in a while, as Coconut Grove shoppers have found out, it is a delectable treat.

1 pound butter, softened	1 16-ounce jar apricot jam
1 pint sour cream	½ cup coconut
2 tablespoons sugar	½ cup walnuts
4 cups flour, sifted	½ cup raisins

Cream the butter, sour cream, and sugar and add the flour. Chill for 4 hours. Then remove the dough from the refrigerator and roll one third of it into an 8-by-20-inch rectangle. Spread a third of the jam, coconut, walnuts, and raisins over half the dough (lengthwise). Fold the dough over and cut it into 2-by-4-inch rectangles. Sprinkle them with sugar and bake in a preheated 350° oven for 40 minutes. Repeat with remaining two thirds, rolled out in the same size segments, or freeze as much dough as you like before rolling it out.

Couronne des Rois

LA MARQUISE, NEW ORLEANS

From the south of France comes this pretty *couronne des rois*, re-created in New Orleans by Maurice Delechelle, whose *salon de thé* is a popular spot with the French Quarter's artists and writers. Any of the decorations for this brioche ring may be used.

4 cups all-purpose flour
1 tablespoon active dry yeast
¼ cup lukewarm water
5 eggs
¼ cup sugar
1 teaspoon salt

½ pound butter
Rock sugar, colored sugar,
  raisins, candied cherries, or
  almonds (for decoration)
Apricot glaze or diluted jam

Sift the flour onto a work surface or into a large bowl and make a well in the middle of it. Mix a little of the flour with the yeast. Add to this the ¼ cup lukewarm water and set the mixture aside to proof. Put four of the eggs, the sugar, salt, and the yeast mixture in the well in the center of the flour and mix it together. Knead the dough until it is elastic. Mix in the butter well. Let the dough rise, covered, for 3 hours at room temperature. Knead it again and refrigerate it for 6 hours. Then remove the dough and shape it into a ball. Push a hole in the center of the ball, making a 12-inch-diameter ring. Let the cake rise, covered, 3 more hours at room temperature. Then brush it with the remaining egg, beaten. Decorate it, brush it with the apricot glaze or diluted jam, and bake it in a preheated 375° oven for 25 minutes.

Desserts

Incredible Chocolate Mousse Cake

THE SILVER PALATE, NEW YORK CITY   *Serves 12 to 16*
   (UPPER WEST SIDE)

Although its elegant line of packaged delicacies is sold at fancy food shops all over the country, The Silver Palate still thinks of itself as a little neighborhood place — a shop where you can pick up brownies like the ones mother used to make. Mother probably never made a chocolate mousse cake like this one.

Clearly a cake for a very special occasion, the recipe involves a mousse, a cake, and a glaze. Make them in the order in which they are given and the whole operation will come out perfectly.

Chocolate Mousse

1 pound chocolate chips
6 tablespoons espresso coffee
6 tablespoons Kahlua (or other
   coffee liqueur)

3 egg yolks
¾ cup heavy cream
6 egg whites
Pinch of salt

Melt the chocolate chips in the top of a double boiler. Add the coffee and the liqueur and stir until smooth. Cool to room temperature.

Add the egg yolks one at a time, stirring after each addition. Set the mixture aside. Whip the cream until firm.

In another bowl, whip the egg whites and a pinch of salt until stiff. Gently fold the egg whites into the cream and then fold the chocolate mixture into the egg white–cream mixture. Pour the mousse into a 1½-quart container and refrigerate until set — about 3 hours. Proceed with the cake.

Chocolate Cake

¾ cup boiling water

½ cup cocoa

1⅔ cups flour

1 tablespoon baking powder

½ teaspoon salt

1⅔ cups sugar

7 "large" eggs, separated

½ cup vegetable oil

1½ teaspoons vanilla extract

1¼ cups apricot preserves

In a small bowl, pour the boiling water over the cocoa, stirring constantly until it is smooth. Set aside and let the mixture come to room temperature.

Sift the dry ingredients together into a large mixing bowl. Pour the egg yolks, oil, vanilla, and cooled chocolate over the dry ingredients. Beat together until they are mixed and smooth.

Whip the egg whites until peaks form and fold them into the batter until just blended. Do not overmix.

Pour the batter into an ungreased 10-inch tube pan with a removable bottom. Bake in a preheated 325° oven for 55 to 60 minutes, or just until the center springs back when touched. Do not overbake, or the cake will be dry.

Let the cake cool in the pan for 30 minutes. Then run a sharp knife around the outside edge. Remove the outside part of the pan, leaving the cake with the bottom and center. Let it cool for another 30 minutes. Then remove the cake in the following manner: Insert a sharp knife between the cake and the bottom of the pan, running the knife clockwise and turning the center counterclockwise to loosen the center part of the cake. Remove the cake from the pan.

Place it bottom side up, and cut it crosswise into four equal layers. Separate so that each layer will cool.

When the layers are almost cool, melt the apricot preserves in a saucepan over low heat. Paint the top of each layer with one fourth of the melted preserves. Allow to cool to room temperature. Proceed with the chocolate glaze and assembly.

Chocolate Glaze

6 tablespoons dark corn syrup
⅓ cup sugar
⅓ cup water

8 ounces unsweetened
 chocolate
3 tablespoons butter

Put the corn syrup, sugar, and water in a saucepan and bring the mixture to a full boil over medium heat. Remove the pan from the heat and stir in the chocolate and butter and whisk until the mixture is smooth. Set it aside to cool for a few minutes as you assemble the cake.

Assembly

Place the bottom layer, apricot side up, on a platter. Spread one third of the mousse over the layer. Place the second layer on the cake and spread with the second third of the mousse. Place the third layer on the cake and spread the remaining mousse over it. Top with the final layer and pour the chocolate glaze over the top and sides of the cake. Decorate the top with apricot slices, if you wish. Refrigerate until ready to serve.

Light Chocolate Cake   *Serves 16 to 20*
LE PETIT CHEF, MINNEAPOLIS

This recipe makes two 10-inch cakes, which you can serve as they are or make considerably richer by using the chocolate mousse recipe that follows as a filling and frosting. To do so, bake the cakes as directed and then, when they are cool, cut them crosswise in halves or thirds.

9 eggs at room temperature
1 cup sugar

¼ cup unsweetened cocoa
1 cup cornstarch

Beat the eggs and sugar together until they reach a ribbonlike consistency. Be patient; this may take 10 minutes or more. Mix the cocoa and cornstarch together. With a spatula, fold them into the egg-sugar mixture. Blend well.

Pour the batter into two greased 10-inch round pans that are at least 3 inches deep. Bake in a preheated 350° oven for 45 minutes, or until the edges shrink from the sides of the pan. Invert the cakes onto wire racks.

Quick Chocolate Mousse

Serves 10

LE PETIT CHEF, MINNEAPOLIS

This is a very handy recipe to know about. It's easy, it uses prepared fudge sauce that can be kept on hand for an emergency, and it also may be used as a frosting and filling for the light chocolate cake (or any other cake).

2 cups heavy cream
1 tablespoon unsweetened
   cocoa

2 cups extra thick fudge
   topping (your own or a
   prepared sauce)

Whip the cream until it is moderately stiff. Mix the cocoa into the fudge topping and fold it completely into the cream. Spoon the mixture into dessert dishes and refrigerate.

Chocolate Grand Marnier Cake   *Serves 12 to 16*

THE CHEF'S GARDEN AND TRUFFLES, NAPLES, FLORIDA

Up above The Chef's Garden in the heart of Olde Naples, an enclave of exclusive shopping elegance, is the café section of the restaurant. Called Truffles, it features a take-out counter of pâtés and terrines and mouth-watering breads and pastries. Chef-owner Tony Ridgway is a former Air Force electronics officer. This smooth-textured cake is one of his most popular creations.

Cake

½ cup butter
1¼ cups sugar
1 teaspoon vanilla extract
2 eggs
2 cups sifted cake flour

¼ teaspoon salt
½ teaspoon baking soda
1½ teaspoons baking powder
½ cup cocoa
1¼ cups chilled coffee

Cream the butter, sugar, and vanilla. Add the eggs one at a time, beating thoroughly after each addition. Sift the dry ingredients together and add to the creamed mixture alternately with the chilled coffee.

Pour into two 8-inch greased and floured cake pans and bake in a preheated 350° oven for 30 to 35 minutes.

Butter Cream

¼ cup water
¾ cup sugar
5 egg yolks

¼ pound unsalted butter,
  softened
Grated zest of 1 orange
3 tablespoons Grand Marnier

Make a syrup of the water and sugar and cook it to 336° on a candy thermometer.

Whip the egg yolks in a mixer set on high and add the hot syrup. The volume will greatly increase. The mixture will be very pale in color and very light and have large air bubbles that will rise to the surface. Cool it completely.

Work the egg yolk mixture into the butter. Add the orange zest and the Grand Marnier and mix thoroughly.

Chocolate Glaze

10 ounces semisweet
  chocolate

1 cup *crème fraîche* (1 tablespoon buttermilk mixed with 1 cup whipping cream)

Gently melt the chocolate and the *crème fraîche* over hot water in a double boiler. Hold it at room temperature (75° to 85°).

Assembly

Cut each of the cake layers crosswise in two, producing four layers. Sprinkle each with a little Grand Marnier. Spread each layer, including the top one, and the sides, with butter cream. Ice the entire cake, being careful to keep the icing smooth. Chill the cake to set the butter cream.

Have the chocolate glaze liquid but not warm. Set the chilled cake on a rack and glaze it with the chocolate. Decorate with rosettes of butter cream and with Mandarin orange slices. If there is leftover glaze, it makes a fine topping for eclairs or cream puffs.

Chestnut and Chocolate Cake

Serves 8 to 10

BAGATELLE, BEVERLY HILLS

No waist watcher should indulge in this extravagant dessert that chef André Pister calls a cake but doesn't actually bake.

1 pound unsweetened chestnut
   purée
½ cup (scant) sugar
3½ ounces semisweet
   chocolate

1 teaspoon vanilla extract
½ cup (scant) unsalted butter
2 tablespoons light rum

Melt the chestnut purée, sugar, and chocolate in the top of a double boiler, stirring with a wooden spoon. Add the vanilla. Remove from stove and add the butter and rum. Pour into a greased 8-by-3½-inch Pyrex pan and let cool. Serve with whipped cream and *crème anglaise.*

Crème Anglaise

1 cup sugar
6 egg yolks

1 teaspoon vanilla extract
2 cups hot milk

Beat the sugar into the egg yolks and vanilla. Gradually add the hot milk. Cook the mixture gently in the top of a double boiler, stirring constantly. When the sauce is smooth and coats a metal mixing spoon, remove it from the stove; to cool the sauce, place the pan in a bowl filled with ice.

Hot Fudge Pudding Cake

Serves 8 to 10

GRETCHEN'S OF COURSE, SEATTLE

This yummy dessert is rich, rich, rich and sweet, sweet, sweet. Served hot and topped with whipped cream or light cream, it is hard to beat.

2 cups flour
4 teaspoons baking powder
½ teaspoon salt
1½ cups sugar
⅓ cup unsweetened cocoa
1 cup milk

4 tablespoons melted butter or margarine
2 cups chopped walnuts
2 cups light brown sugar
½ cup unsweetened cocoa
3½ cups boiling water

In a bowl, sift together the flour, baking powder, salt, sugar, and the ⅓ cup cocoa. Stir in the milk, butter, and nuts. The mixture will be quite thick. Spread it in a 9-by-13-inch baking dish or other shallow casserole. Sprinkle over it the combined brown sugar and ½ cup cocoa and pour boiling water over all. Bake in a preheated 350° oven for 45 minutes. Bubbles will appear around the edges. The top will be firm but will "float." Serve warm.

THE COMMISSARY

Chocolate Cheese Cake

Serves 12

THE CHEF'S GARDEN AND TRUFFLES, NAPLES, FLORIDA

This melt-in-your-mouth chocolate cheese cake is topped with pecans and coconut. Baker Jim Schaefer created it to meet a popular demand for a dessert that was "ultra-rich and ultra-sinful."

Crust

1¼ cups graham cracker
  crumbs

2 tablespoons sugar
3 tablespoons melted butter

Preheat the oven to 350°. Mix the crumbs, sugar, and butter, and press the mixture evenly into the bottom of an ungreased 10-inch springform. Bake for 10 minutes. Cool to make ready for the filling. Reduce the oven temperature to 300°.

Cake

11 ounces cream cheese, at
  room temperature
1 cup sugar

¼ cup unsweetened cocoa
2 teaspoons vanilla extract
3 eggs

Cream the cheese using an electric mixer. Add the sugar and cocoa. Mix until very light and fluffy. Add the vanilla and the eggs, one at a time, beating after each addition. Pour the mixture into the graham cracker crust.

Place the cheese cake in a water bath that goes halfway up the sides of the springform. Bake for approximately 1 hour, or until the center of the cake is firm. Remove the cheese cake from the oven and let it cool to room temperature.

Topping

2 tablespoons butter
⅓ cup heavy cream
2 tablespoons brown sugar
2 egg yolks

½ teaspoon vanilla extract
½ cup chopped pecans
½ cup flaked coconut

Cook the butter, cream, brown sugar, and egg yolks over moderate direct heat, stirring constantly until the mixture has thickened. Remove it from the heat. Stir in the vanilla, pecans, and coconut. Cool.

Assembly

Spread the cooled cheese cake with the topping. Refrigerate it for 3 hours. Then remove it from the springform; be sure to run a dull knife around the edge of the pan before trying to remove the cake. Refrigerate until ready to serve.

Cheese Cake

E.A.T., NEW YORK CITY (UPPER EAST SIDE)

At E.A.T. the confections are delicious — enormous shortbread cookies, pound cake, almond cake. E.A.T. co-owner and master chef Eli Zabar creates them all — with an imaginative dash of this and a dollop of that. This cheese cake with browned butter is a neighborhood favorite.

1 pound cream cheese, at room temperature
3 eggs
½ teaspoon vanilla extract
½ cup sugar

3 tablespoons browned melted butter
Toasted bread crumbs mixed with butter, sufficient to line the pan

Preheat the oven to 350°. Beat the cream cheese in a mixer until soft. Add the eggs one at a time, beating after each addition. Add the vanilla and beat briefly. Add the sugar and beat slowly for 10 minutes. Add the browned (almost burned) butter. Beat until mixed. Pour the batter into a 6-inch pudding pan that has been lined with the toasted bread crumbs mixed with melted butter. Put the pudding pan in a water bath that reaches halfway up the sides and bake the cake for 45 minutes. Serve chilled or at room temperature.

Praline Cheese Cake

Serves 8 to 12

PASTA PRESTO, KANSAS CITY, MISSOURI

Pasta Presto specializes, as its name suggests, in fresh pasta, but it sells homemade vinegars and fine olive oils, bread and sausages, and the richest of desserts, too. It is located in Westport, the oldest part of Kansas City, not far from where the Santa Fe and Oregon trails once began. In trail days, Westport was one of the last places to buy supplies for the trek west. Today, Pasta Presto is the place to purchase the supplies for a gourmet dinner party.

Crust

1¼ cups graham cracker
    crumbs
¼ cup sugar

¼ cup pecans, toasted and
    finely chopped, but not
    ground
¼ cup melted butter

Combine the crumbs, sugar, pecans, and butter. Press the mixture into a 9- or 10-inch springform. Bake for 10 minutes in a preheated 300° oven.

Filling

1½ pounds cream cheese,
    softened
1 cup brown sugar
5⅓ ounces evaporated milk

2 tablespoons flour
1½ teaspoons vanilla extract
3 eggs

Combine the cream cheese, brown sugar, evaporated milk, flour, and vanilla in the bowl of an electric mixer; blend them well. Add the eggs, one at a time, mixing well after each addition. Pour the mixture into the crust and bake for 50 minutes in a preheated 325° oven.

When you are ready to serve the cheese cake, paint the top of it with maple syrup and/or decorate the top with toasted pecans.

Apple Cake

A MOVEABLE FEAST, PHILADELPHIA

After seven years of catering to the tastes of the academic community of University City from their old pharmacy shop on Spruce Street, the owners of A Moveable Feast have opened a branch in the Reading Terminal Market, more convenient to the rest of Philadelphia. This apple cake, and everything else, though, is still prepared at the Spruce Street shop.

2 cups sugar
3 eggs
1¼ cups salad oil
¼ teaspoon salt
¼ cup orange juice
3 cups sifted flour
1 teaspoon baking soda

1 teaspoon cinnamon
1 teaspoon vanilla extract
1 cup peeled and chopped raw apples
1 cup shredded coconut
1 cup chopped nuts

Sauce

6 tablespoons butter
1 cup sugar

½ teaspoon baking soda
½ cup buttermilk

Mix together all the ingredients up to the apples, in the order given. Then mix in, with a spoon, the apples, coconut, and nuts.

Pour the batter into a greased and floured tube pan. Bake in a preheated 325° oven for 1½ hours.

When the cake is almost done, prepare the sauce. Melt the butter and stir in all the other ingredients. Bring the mixture to a rolling boil. Pour the sauce over the hot cake while it is still in the pan. Let it stand for at least one hour before turning it out.

Carrot Cake

McMEAD'S, MIAMI, FLORIDA

At McMead's, a supersophisticated, supersolicitous catering service and gourmet take-out shop in the Coconut Grove section of Miami, unsophisticated carrot cake is an all-time favorite.

4 eggs	1 tablespoon allspice
2 cups sugar	1 tablespoon ground cinnamon
1½ cups vegetable oil	2 cups all-purpose flour
2 teaspoons baking soda	3 cups grated carrots

Beat the eggs and gradually add the sugar, beating thoroughly. Slowly add the vegetable oil. Add the baking soda, allspice, and cinnamon. Fold in the flour and then the grated carrots. Bake in two 10-inch greased and floured cake pans in a preheated 350° oven for 30 to 40 minutes. Frost with a cream cheese icing and top the cake with walnuts.

Cream Cheese Frosting

3 cups softened cream cheese	1 cup confectioners' sugar, sifted
1 cup softened butter	⅓ cup frozen orange juice (undiluted)

Beat together the cream cheese, butter, sugar, and orange juice until smooth and of spreading consistency.

Strawberry Tart

DEAN & DeLUCA, NEW YORK CITY (SoHo)

Ideally, one would like to shop at Dean & DeLuca with a weekend guest list of 500 close friends and a piece of the Defense Department's budget. Actually, the attraction of this lively food store is such that some New Yorkers travel long distances just to pick up a few groceries. It does take will power, though, not to come away with such extras as this strawberry tart.

Pâte Brisée

¼ cup butter
1 cup pastry flour
⅛ teaspoon salt
1 tablespoon sugar

2 tablespoons shortening
1 tablespoon sour cream
Ice water (if necessary)

All the ingredients should be very cold.

Cut butter into small pieces and set it aside.

Sift the flour, salt, and sugar together in a mixing bowl. Add the butter, shortening, and sour cream, working all together quickly with your fingertips. If it doesn't come together quickly, add a few drops of ice water until the mixture forms a doughlike consistency. Handle the dough as little as possible. Wrap it in plastic wrap and refrigerate it for half an hour.

Preheat the oven to 400°.

Put an 8-inch pastry ring on a cookie sheet. Roll out the dough on a marble slab or a lightly floured board, sprinkling a little flour as you work to keep it from sticking. Lay the dough inside the pastry ring, pressing the edges to the sides of the ring with a fork. Prick several holes in the bottom of the shell and cover it with wax paper. Fill the paper with dried beans to hold the shell down. Bake for 20 minutes. Remove the paper and the beans and bake for another 5 minutes, or until the bottom of the shell is dry. Cool on a rack.

Apricot Glaze

½ cup apricot preserves   ¼ cup brandy

Combine the preserves and brandy in the top of a double boiler. Cook until the preserves loosen up and are piping hot. Force through a sieve and reheat in the double boiler.

Brush the bottom and sides of the cooled pastry shell with the glaze. Set the shell and extra glaze aside.

Crème Pâtissière

¼ cup sugar
2 tablespoons cornstarch
Pinch of salt
½ cup milk
½ cup heavy cream

2½ egg yolks (to get half a yolk, beat a whole yolk and divide it in half)
¾ teaspoon vanilla extract

Combine the sugar, cornstarch, and salt in the top of a double boiler. Stir in half of the milk and mix well.

Heat the remainder of the milk and the cream and add gradually to the cornstarch mixture, stirring well.

Beat the egg yolks and add them gradually, stirring constantly. Cook until thick, continuing to stir. Remove from the heat. Cool slightly and add the vanilla. Chill. Whisk occasionally to prevent a skin from forming.

Assembly

1 quart strawberries

Wipe and hull the strawberries and set them aside. Fill the pastry shell half full with the *crème pâtissière*. Place it in the refrigerator for a few minutes to set.

Starting at the outside of the shell, arrange the whole strawberries on the *crème pâtissière* until the shell is full. Brush the strawberries with the remainder of the apricot glaze and let the tart sit for at least 10 minutes before serving. It will keep without refrigeration for 24 hours.

Frozen Key Lime Pie
Serves 6

SI BON, SANIBEL, FLORIDA

> When Michigander Ginger Carter opened Si Bon in 1977, she was not only blazing culinary trails on Sanibel Island, a stretch of sheller's paradise and wildlife refuge, she was blazing trails for the entire west coast of Florida, where gourmet take-out shops were then an unknown convenience. Reflecting her affection for her adopted state, she developed her own version of that Florida favorite, the Key lime pie. If you can't get Key limes, use ordinary limes.

Crust

1¼ cups graham cracker crumbs

¼ cup sugar
¼ cup softened butter

Mix all the ingredients and press them into a greased 9-inch pie tin. Bake the crust for 10 minutes in a preheated 350° oven and cool it to room temperature.

Filling

5 eggs, separated
1 cup sugar

⅔ cup fresh lime juice
2 teaspoons grated lemon rind
Salt to taste

Beat the egg yolks in the top of a double boiler until very thick. Gradually beat in ¾ cup sugar until the mixture turns pale yellow and is thick enough to form a ribbon when dribbled off the beater. Add the lime juice and lemon rind. Stir over simmering water until the mixture coats a spoon, but do not let it boil. Cool to room temperature.

Beat the egg whites with a pinch of salt until soft peaks form. Gradually add the remaining ¼ cup sugar and beat until the whites are stiff and shiny. Whisk one third of the whites into the cooled yolk mixture and then fold in the rest. Fill the cooled pie shell. Bake for 15 minutes in a preheated 350° oven. Cool. Chill in refrigerator and then freeze. When the pie is frozen, cover it with plastic wrap.

Topping

1½ cups whipped cream

1 lime, thinly sliced
Sugar

About 10 minutes before serving the pie, cover it with whipped cream and decorate it with lime slices dipped in sugar.

SUZANNE'S

Lemony Raisin Pie

Serves 8

GOODIES TO GO, LEXINGTON, MASSACHUSETTS

A never-fail pie crust is among the attractions of this simple sweet-tart pie. At congenial Goodies, customers chat with the bakers and ask them for tips as the professionals roll out their dough.

Filling

1 tablespoon all-purpose flour
1 cup sugar
1 tablespoon melted butter
1 teaspoon lemon juice

Grated rind of 1 lemon
1 cup cold water
1 cup raisins (puffed, seeded muscats are especially good)

Combine the flour and sugar in a saucepan. Stir in the melted butter, lemon juice, and lemon rind. Add the cold water and raisins. Cook over medium-low heat until thick, stirring constantly. Set aside while you make the crust.

Crust

½ cup vegetable shortening
½ cup lard
3 cups all-purpose flour
1 teaspoon salt

1 egg, beaten
5 tablespoons cold water
1 tablespoon vinegar

Cut the shortening and lard into the flour. Mix in the other ingredients and roll out half the dough. Put it in a greased 9-inch pie plate, add the filling, and top with the second crust. Bake in a preheated 450° oven for 20 minutes; turn the oven down to 375° and bake for 40 minutes more, until the crust is golden brown.

Raspberry Tart

Serves 8

MANGIA, WEST LOS ANGELES

When raspberries are in season, what could be better than a sweet, fragrant raspberry tart spilling over with the ripe red fruit? At Mangia, even the movie folk go off their diets for a slice.

Tart Shell

1 cup all-purpose flour, sifted	2 egg yolks
⅔ cup pastry flour, sifted	1 teaspoon vanilla extract
¼ cup sugar	½ teaspoon water
6 tablespoons unsalted butter	

Combine all the dry ingredients. Add the butter, egg yolks, vanilla, and water and mix well by hand or with an electric mixer. Gather into a ball and refrigerate until it is solid.

Filling

¾ cup unsalted butter	¼ cup flour
3 eggs	2 pints (or more) raspberries
1 cup sugar	Raspberry jam

Brown the butter over high heat until speckles appear on the surface. Mix the eggs, sugar, and flour with a whisk in a medium-sized bowl. Add the hot butter and whisk it in.

Roll out the dough and lay it in a 9-inch pie pan. Scatter the raspberries in the tart shell and pour the filling on top. Bake the tart in a preheated 350° oven for 45 minutes to 1 hour, or until firm to the touch. Brush the top with a thin coating of raspberry jam after you remove the tart from the oven. Arrange more whole raspberries on top, if desired.

Apple Tart

MITCHELL COBEY CUISINE, CHICAGO

"Simple as pie," Mitchell Cobey quips, as he talks of this delicious French-style apple tart made, preferably, with firm Granny Smith or Delicious apples, and embellished with raisins marinated in brandy.

Crust

1⅓ cups all-purpose flour   ½ cup unsalted butter
1 tablespoon sugar   ¼ cup water

Sift together the flour and sugar. Cut in the butter. Sprinkle the water onto this mixture and form the dough into a ball. Roll it out on a floured surface and lay in a greased 10-inch fluted tart pan. Put the shell in the refrigerator and chill it for 1 hour. Line the shell with foil or parchment paper and sprinkle a handful of beans in it; bake the shell in a preheated 400° oven until it is slightly browned, 7 or 8 minutes. Remove the beans. Meanwhile, prepare the filling.

Filling

6 Granny Smith or red   ½ cup raisins marinated for 2
  Delicious apples, peeled,   hours or more in ⅓ cup
  cored, and sliced   brandy
Juice of 1 lemon   Butter to taste
1 cup plus 1 tablespoon   Sufficient apricot preserves for
  granulated sugar   glaze (about ⅓ cup)
1 teaspoon ground cinnamon

Put three of the peeled, cored, and sliced apples into a pan with the lemon juice and the 1 cup of sugar and cook the mixture over low heat until it is thick. Stir in the cinnamon and the raisins. Spread this

212

mixture on the bottom of the tart shell. Top with slices of the other three apples. Sprinkle the top with the tablespoon of sugar and dot it with butter. Bake it in a preheated 450° oven until the apples begin to brown, between 20 and 30 minutes. Finally, melt the apricot preserves with a little water over low heat. Coat the top of the tart with this glaze. Serve warm or at room temperature.

Ginger Pear Pie
Serves 6

REBECCA'S, BOSTON

The combination of sweet fresh pears, sour cream, brown sugar, and spices is unbeatable served in a flaky pie shell. If this pie seems too filling for the end of a meal, try it at a coffee klatch or tea.

1 unbaked 9-inch pie shell
3 Anjou pears
2 eggs, beaten
⅓ cup sugar
¼ teaspoon salt
¼ teaspoon ground ginger
Pinch of nutmeg

½ teaspoon grated lemon rind
¼ teaspoon vanilla extract
¼ teaspoon almond extract
1 cup sour cream
Brown sugar crumbs (see recipe below)

Partially bake the pie shell (in a preheated 350° oven for about 7 minutes), making sure to prick it in several places before cooking it. Peel the pears and cut them into bite-size pieces. Stir the other ingredients, except the brown sugar crumbs, into the beaten eggs. Pour half of this mixture into the pie shell and arrange the pears on top. Pour the other half of the mixture over the pears and top the pie with the brown sugar crumbs. Bake the pie in a preheated 325° oven until the filling is set and the top is golden brown, approximately 45 minutes.

Brown Sugar Crumbs

¼ cup flour
3 tablespoons brown sugar

2 tablespoons butter
Pinch of nutmeg

Using a fork, combine all the ingredients until they reach a crumb-like consistency.

Lemon Tart

Serves 8

LA BELLE CUISINE, GLENCOE, ILLINOIS

La Belle Cuisine looks like a French country café with flowered wallpaper and hand-painted tiles on its tables, and its customers enjoy the sunny, homespun atmosphere. But sometimes they really would rather be at home, and for those times the restaurant's owners, Lee and Lucie Keating, offer entrées, soups, pies, and tarts to take out. This lemon tart is always a favorite.

Crust

½ cup butter
¼ cup sugar

1 egg
1 cup all-purpose flour, sifted

Work the butter with the sugar until the mixture is smooth. Beat in the egg and add the flour. Make a ball of the dough and place it between two pieces of floured wax paper. Flatten it into an 11-inch circle. Refrigerate it while you make the filling.

Filling

3 eggs
½ cup sugar
⅓ cup fresh lemon juice

½ cup softened butter
¾ cup ground almonds

214

Whip the eggs, sugar, and lemon juice together. When the sugar is dissolved, add the butter and cream the mixture. Add the almonds.

Grease a 9-inch cake tin with a removable bottom and lay the dough in it, patching any tears with bits of leftover dough. Cut any excess dough off the edges. Pour the filling into the crust and bake the tart in a preheated 375° oven for 40 to 45 minutes.

Berries' Favorite Shortcake
Serves 6

GOODIES TO GO, LEXINGTON, MASSACHUSETTS

This is an exceptionally rich shortcake to go under your favorite summer berries.

2 cups all-purpose flour
4 teaspoons baking powder
½ teaspoon salt
2 tablespoons sugar

½ cup butter, melted
1 egg
½ cup cream

Mix all the ingredients together and spread the batter into a greased 8-inch pan. Bake in a preheated 450° oven for 10 or 15 minutes, until golden brown.

Les Chefettes
Gourmet Cookshop

Visidantine

DÉLICES LA CÔTE BASQUE, NEW YORK CITY
 (UPPER EAST SIDE)

When Guy Pascal, the miracle-making pastry chef who founded Délices la Côte Basque five years ago, was a child growing up in Avignon, France, his farmer father was determined that Guy would be a pastry chef. Guy was equally determined to be a ballet dancer. As it turned out, he ended up both, performing as a dancer in Paris and Las Vegas, and as a pastry chef in Las Vegas and New York. But these days, when there are lines at his Lexington Avenue café–pastry shop on weekend mornings, the stage has had to be abandoned in favor of the kitchen. There he produces delights like this almond tart.

Crust

2 cups flour
½ cup granulated sugar
2 eggs

½ teaspoon vanilla extract
½ teaspoon lemon juice
¼ pound butter, cut into small
 pieces

Filling

¼ pound butter at room
 temperature
⅔ cup granulated sugar
1⅓ cups ground blanched
 almonds

3 "large" eggs
1 tablespoon dark rum
1 cup thinly sliced blanched
 almonds

Glaze

¼ cup apricot preserves

2 tablespoons water

There are two methods of making the crust, in a food processor or by hand. If you use a food processor, place the flour and the sugar in its container and start the motor. Then, one at a time, add the eggs, blending them in. Then add the vanilla and lemon juice and blend. Add the butter and continue blending until a workable dough forms.

To make the dough by hand, spoon the flour onto a marble or Formica surface and make a well in the center of the mound of flour. Add the sugar to the well and break the eggs at a point where the sugar and flour meet. Add the vanilla and lemon juice to the eggs. With your fingers, blend the sugar, eggs, lemon juice, and vanilla. Add the butter and start working the center ingredients while gradually bringing the flour into the center mass and working it in. Knead well, pushing the mixture away from you with the base of your hand, then scraping it back, kneading and scraping back again until the dough is well worked.

Roll the dough into a circle on a lightly floured board. Line a 9-inch quiche pan with a removable bottom with the dough. Build up the sides slightly. Prick the bottom and refrigerate. (Any leftover dough may be used to make cookies.) Preheat the oven to 400°.

To prepare the filling, cream the butter in an electric mixer. Combine the sugar and ground almonds. Add about one third of this mixture to the butter along with one egg. Beat well. Add another third of the sugar-almond mixture and one more egg and again beat well. Add the final third and the last egg and blend well. Beat in the rum.

Spoon and scrape this mixture into the prepared quiche pan and sprinkle it with the sliced almonds. Bake for 35 minutes. Remove the tart from the ring.

To prepare the glaze, melt the apricot preserves with the water over low heat, stirring constantly. Spread this over the top of the cooled tart.

Gâteau Pithiviers

Serves 12

LA MARQUISE, NEW ORLEANS

This confection of puff pastry, filled with a *frangipane* of almond paste, butter, and eggs, was named for the French town of Pithiviers near Orléans. It is a favorite with tourists and locals alike, who pause to sit in La Marquise's Spanish-style courtyard in New Orleans's French Quarter.

Filling

2 ounces very finely crushed almonds (approximately ½ cup)

¼ cup sugar
4 tablespoons salted butter
1 egg

Mix all the ingredients well and refrigerate them.

Pastry

1 pound bleached all-purpose flour
6 tablespoons salted butter
½ teaspoon salt

1 cup cold water
1 egg
11 ounces (2 sticks plus 6 tablespoons) salted butter

Mix all the ingredients except the egg and the 11 ounces of butter, making sure that the dough is smooth and thoroughly blended. Roll out the dough as thinly as possible on a floured board, slathering the top with some of the 11 ounces of butter, and fold it into thirds. Refrigerate it for 2 to 3 hours. Repeat this rolling and folding five times, slathering the top of the pastry with more of the 11 ounces of butter each time, then refrigerating the dough again for 2 to 3 hours.

218

Finally, remove the dough from the refrigerator and cut it in half. Roll out each half very thin. Use a 10-inch cake pan to lightly impress a circle on one sheet of the dough. Fill the area inside the circle with the almond filling. Cover it with the other sheet of thinly rolled dough. Again, press a cake pan upside down over the cake, taking care not to cut through the pastry, for this seals the filling inside the cake. Use a small, sharp knife to scallop the edges of the pastry. Discard any excess.

Using a sharp knife, incise crescent designs radiating from the center of the cake to the edge. Brush the top with a well-beaten egg and bake in a preheated 375° oven for 40 minutes.

Pere Ripieni (Stuffed Pears)   *Serves 6*

VIVANDE, SAN FRANCISCO

Desserts need not be complicated or overly rich to be the satisfying finishing touch to a meal, Carlo Middione of Vivande believes. His pears stuffed with Gorgonzola have proved a most successful dessert. In a pinch, Danish bleu may be substituted for the Gorgonzola.

6 Comice (preferable) or Bosc pears, ripe but very firm
Lemon juice
6 tablespoons unsalted butter
¾ cup imported Gorgonzola cheese
½ cup (or more) crushed walnuts

Peel the pears. Cut them in half, but leave the stem attached to one side. Scoop out the seeds and some of the pulp to make room for the stuffing. Brush or rub the pears all over with lemon juice to prevent them from turning brown.

Cream the butter and cheese together with half the walnuts.

Stuff the pears and put the two halves of each pear together. The cheese mixture will make them stick together. Sprinkle or press any remaining walnuts on the pears, or roll them in toasted finely ground almonds. Garnish each pear with a mint leaf, if you wish, and serve chilled.

Poached Pears on a Bed of Apple Purée

WASHINGTON MARKET, NEW YORK CITY (TRIBECA)   *Serves 6*

Huge windows, high ceilings, and wide aisles make this old building of the original Washington Market a perfect backdrop for good food handsomely displayed. The young owners, Jeanne Lee and Ann Wagenknecht, have turned this into a food shop that's worth a visit even if you are not in the neighborhood. They have an artistic touch with the presentation of food, as this dish demonstrates.

3 to 4 cups water
2 cups dry red wine
1½ cups sugar
1 cinnamon stick
3 pears (Bosc, Comice, or Anjou)

12 apples (preferably McIntosh)
6 tablespoons unsalted butter
2 tablespoons pear brandy
2 ounces finely chopped walnuts (for garnish)

Using a nonaluminum pan, bring the water, wine, and sugar to a simmer. Add the cinnamon stick.

Peel the pears, cut them in half, and remove the seeds. Add the pears to the liquid and simmer slowly until they are tender — approximately 30 minutes.

Remove the pears from the liquid and set them aside. Boil down the liquid until it becomes a glaze. If necessary, add a little more sugar. Set aside.

Peel and core the apples and cut them into quarters. Put them in a saucepan with a cup of water and the butter. Cook until they are puréed, stirring often. Add the pear brandy and cool.

To serve, put the purée into individual bowls or dessert dishes. Place a pear half flat side down on the purée, and spoon the glaze over the pears. Garnish with the chopped walnuts.

Eugénie   *Serves 10 to 12*
DÉLICES LA CÔTE BASQUE, NEW YORK CITY
(UPPER EAST SIDE)

Strawberries and cream combined in any fashion are delicious; combined this way at Délices la Côte Basque, they are especially delicious.

1 pint ripe strawberries plus
  six more for garnish
4 tablespoons kirsch or
  framboise
3 cups heavy cream

5 tablespoons sugar
2 tablespoons unflavored
  gelatin
¼ cup cold water

Pick over the berries and hull them. Rinse them well, drain, and pat dry. Cut the pint of berries into ⅛-inch pieces and place them in a bowl. Add 1 tablespoon of the kirsch or framboise and set aside.

Lightly butter an 8-cup soufflé dish and refrigerate it. Beat the cream with a wire whisk or electric beater, and as it begins to stiffen, gradually beat in 3 tablespoons of the sugar. Continue beating until the cream is stiff.

Soften the gelatin and water in a small saucepan and heat, stirring, until the gelatin dissolves. Scrape this into a large mixing bowl and immediately add 1 cup of the whipped cream, stirring rapidly with a whisk to blend it well. Beat in the remaining 2 tablespoons of sugar and the strawberries and stir.

Add the remaining cream and fold it in with a rubber spatula. Spoon it into the prepared mold. Refrigerate it for several hours or until set. When it is ready to serve, dip the mold into a basin of hot water, remove, and dip again; remove and dip a third time. Place a round serving dish over the mold, invert the dish, and unmold the Eugénie. Garnish it with the remaining strawberries, left whole or cut in half.

Poached Pears in Chocolate Sauce Serves 6
CYNTHIA CARISEO CAFÉ, PHILADELPHIA

The dress-designing business was slow and her friends kept telling her she was an "incredible" cook, so Cynthia Cariseo had a thousand flyers printed up offering her services as a caterer for private parties. Within three months, she had earned enough to finance a summer course at La Varenne in Paris. That was in 1979, and since then Cynthia's food career has flourished. In addition to running her café and take-out shop, she gives 5-minute cooking demonstrations on local television every Monday morning.

With this wonderful poaching liquid, these pears don't really need the chocolate sauce, but if you like your lilies gilded, this is a great way to go.

3 cups water
1 cup red wine
1 cup raisins
1 tablespoon ground cloves
1 tablespoon ground cinnamon
1 orange, sliced

6 pears, peeled
6 ounces chocolate chips
¼ cup water, heavy cream, or
  poaching liquid
Raisins from poaching liquid

Put the water, wine, raisins, spices, and orange slices in a saucepan and bring to a boil. Lower the heat and simmer for a few minutes before adding the pears. Poach the pears until they are tender. Drain and set aside.

Combine in the top of a double boiler the chocolate chips, liquid, and raisins. Pour over the pears or serve on the side.

Apricot Mousse

Serves 8

LES CHEFETTES, GREAT NECK, LONG ISLAND

This is both a healthful and delicious party dessert — albeit a trifle hard on the waistline, but, as its creators say, you don't eat it every day.

1 box (11 or 12 ounces) dried
  apricots
⅓ cup plus ½ cup granulated
  sugar
6 eggs, separated
4 tablespoons cognac

1 tablespoon unflavored gelatin
¼ cup cold water
3 tablespoons confectioners'
  sugar (optional)
2 cups heavy cream

In a saucepan, cook the apricots with the ⅓ cup sugar for 15 to 20 minutes in water that just covers them. Purée the apricots and the liquid in a blender or food processor and set aside.

In an electric mixer, beat the egg yolks with the ½ cup sugar until they are thick and lemon-colored. Add the apricot purée and the cognac. Dissolve the gelatin in the cold water and set it in a pan of simmering water until it is clear and liquid. In a thin stream, add the gelatin mixture to the apricot mixture while the beaters are on medium speed. Set the mixture aside.

Beat the egg whites until they are stiff and glossy and hold firm peaks. Fold them into the apricot mixture. Taste, and if the mixture is too tart, add the optional confectioners' sugar when beating the cream.

Beat the cream until whipped, and fold 1½ cups of it into the purée. Save ½ cup for decoration. Pour the mousse into a 2-quart bowl and refrigerate for several hours. Decorate with the additional whipped cream, and serve.

Baklava
Serves about 35

ALESCI'S INTERNATIONAL FOODS, CINCINNATI

A remarkable variety of international breads and pastries is made in the bakery of this food shop, including Italian cakes, German sourdough rye breads, hoagie rolls, and this baklava.

4 cups chopped walnuts
½ cup sugar
1 teaspoon cinnamon
½ teaspoon nutmeg

1 pound melted butter
1 pound frozen phyllo leaves, thawed

Syrup

2½ cups sugar
2½ cups water
1 cup honey

1 cinnamon stick
5 or 6 cloves
1 tablespoon lemon juice

Combine the walnuts, sugar, cinnamon, and nutmeg in a bowl and set aside.

Brush a 9-by-13-inch baking dish with melted butter. Place ten phyllo leaves in the dish, brushing each of them with the melted butter.

Spread half of the nut mixture on the leaves. Cover with three more leaves, each brushed with butter. Spread on the remaining nut mixture. Place the remaining leaves, each brushed with melted butter, on top. Cut the baklava into squares or diamonds before you bake it. Bake in a preheated 375° oven for 45 minutes, or until the pastry is light brown.

Prepare the syrup by placing all the ingredients in a saucepan and bringing them to a boil, then simmering for 10 minutes. Let the baklava cool in its pan. Then pour the warm syrup over it.

Strawberries Olé   *Serves 6 to 8*
THE DELI AT YBOR SQUARE, TAMPA, FLORIDA

No take-out food shop is likely to boast such historic surroundings as The Deli at Ybor Square. It is in a massive brick building that once served as a cigar factory and warehouse and lies just across from the park honoring José Martí, the hero of the Cuban liberation. A few yards away in reborn Ybor Square is Rough Riders, a restaurant filled with memorabilia from the Spanish-American War, when Tampa served as a staging area for the thousands of troops training for the invasion of Mexico.

Rough Riders is where Deli owner Tina Thomas started her culinary career serving Bull Moose Burgers. Now her more sophisticated creations include this creamy dessert.

Crust

½ cup butter   ¼ cup powdered sugar
1 cup sifted all-purpose flour

Blend these ingredients in a food processor. Then roll out or press the dough into a 9-by-12-inch pan and bake it in a preheated 325° oven for 20 to 30 minutes, or until golden brown. Remove it from the oven and let it cool.

Filling

8 ounces cream cheese   2 pints fresh strawberries
1¼ cups granulated sugar   3 tablespoons powdered sugar

Cream the cream cheese and the granulated sugar and spread this mixture over the cooled crust. Wash and hull the strawberries and toss them with the powdered sugar. Spread them over the cream cheese mixture and chill. To serve, cut into squares.

The Shops and Their Addresses

A la Carte at Gilliewrinkles
28 Main Street
Cold Spring Harbor, New York
  11724
(516) 367-9259 or
(516) 549-3849

Abbondanza
1647 Second Avenue
New York, New York 10028
(212) 879-6060

Alesci's International Foods
3866 Paxton Road
Cincinnati, Ohio 45209
(513) 321-8100

The American Café Market
1219 Wisconsin Avenue N.W.
Washington, D.C. 20007
(202) 337-4264
    and
227 Massachusetts Avenue N.E.
Washington, D.C. 20002
(202) 547-8504
    and
301 South Light Street
Baltimore, Maryland 21202
(301) 962-8817

Bagatelle
8690 Wilshire Blvd.
Beverly Hills, California 90211
(213) 659-0782

Balducci's
424 Avenue of the Americas
New York, New York 10011
(212) 673-2600

La Belle Cuisine
378 Park Avenue
Glencoe, Illinois 60022
(312) 835-4720

The Black Forest
1759 Massachusetts Avenue
Cambridge, Massachusetts
  02140
(617) 661-6706

Campbell & Co.'s
  "A Matter of Taste"
500 East Spanish River
  Boulevard
Boca Raton, Florida 33431
(305) 368-2772

Caviar Etcetera
Jericho Turnpike and
   Woodbury Road
Woodbury, New York 11797
(516) 367-3900

The Chaplain's Pantry
110 Tacoma Avenue North
Tacoma, Washington 98402
(206) 627-2213

The Charcuterie
55 Washington Street
Wellesley, Massachusetts
   02181
(617) 237-6995

Les Chefettes
501 Middle Neck Road
Great Neck, New York 11023
(516) 466-4022

The Chef's Garden and Truffles
1300 Third Street South
Naples, Florida 33939
(813) 262-5500

Complete Cuisine Ltd.
322 South Main Street
Ann Arbor, Michigan 48104
(313) 662-0046

Cynthia Cariseo Café
1716 Sansom Street
Philadelphia, Pennsylvania
   19103
(215) 546-7887

Dean & DeLuca
121 Prince Street
New York, New York 10012
(212) 254-7774

The Deli at Ybor Square
8th Avenue and 13th Street
Tampa, Florida 33605
(813) 242-0601

Délices la Côte Basque
1032 Lexington Avenue
New York, New York 10021
(212) 535-3311

Demarchelier
1460 Lexington Avenue
New York, New York 10028
(212) 722-6600

E.A.T.
867 Madison Avenue
New York, New York 10021
(212) 879-4017
      and
1064 Madison Avenue
New York, New York 10028
(212) 879-4017

Fête Accomplie
3714 Macomb Street N.W.
Washington, D.C. 20016
(202) 363-9511

Fettuccine Bros.
2100 Larkin
San Francisco, California 94109
(415) 441-2281

The Fishmonger
252 Huron Avenue
Cambridge, Massachusetts
    02138
(617) 661-4834

Formaggio Kitchen
244 Huron Avenue
Cambridge, Massachusetts
    02138
(617) 354-4750

The Fruit Lady
1717 Walnut Street
Philadelphia, Pennsylvania
    19103
(215) 568-6637

Goodies to Go
1734 Massachusetts Avenue
Lexington, Massachusetts
    02173
(617) 863-1704

The Gourmet Grocer
5321 West 94th Terrace
Prairie Village, Kansas 66207
(913) 381-7999

Gourmet Pasta
156C Middle Neck Road
Great Neck, New York 11021
(516) 487-0088
        and
1470 Second Avenue
New York, New York 10021
(212) 737-8750

Gretchen's Of Course
94 Stewart Avenue
Seattle, Washington 98101
(206) 621-9133

*Jim Jamail & Sons Food
    Market*
3114 Kirby Drive
Houston, Texas 77098
(713) 523-5535

Jonathan's
15 Wall Street
Huntington, New York 11743
(516) 549-0055

*Kenessey Gourmets
    Internationale*
403 West Belmont Avenue
Chicago, Illinois 60657
(312) 929-7500

Lisi's Hors d'Oeuvre Bakery
954 West Diversey
Chicago, Illinois 60614
(312) 327-3455

Maggie Gin's Pure and Fresh
Chinese Country Cooking
Restaurant
1234 Main Street
St. Helena, California 94574
(707) 963-9764

Mangia
10543 West Pico Boulevard
Rancho Park, California 90064
(213) 470-1952

marché Gourmet
At The Borgata
6166 North Scottsdale Road,
   Suite 700
Scottsdale, Arizona 85253
(602) 998-0990

The Market of the Commissary
130 South 17th Street
Philadelphia, Pennsylvania
   19103
(215) 568-8055

Le Marmiton
1327 Montana Avenue
Santa Monica, California 90403
(213) 393-7716

La Marquise
625 Rue Chartres
New Orleans, Louisiana 70130
(504) 524-0420

McMead's
3356 Virginia Street
Coconut Grove, Florida 33133
(305) 443-0100

Mitchell Cobey Cuisine
100 East Walton
Chicago, Illinois 60611
(312) 944-3411

A Moveable Feast
4443 Spruce Street
Philadelphia, Pennsylvania
   19104
(215) 387-0676

Neuman & Bogdonoff
1385 Third Avenue
New York, New York 10021
(212) 861-0303

The Oakville Grocery
Company
1555 Pacific Avenue
San Francisco, California 94109
(415) 885-4411

Ouisie's Table and the
Traveling Brown Bag
Lunch Co.
1708 Sunset Boulevard
Houston, Texas 77005
(713) 528-2264

Pasta, Inc.
2805 M Street N.W.
Washington, D.C. 20007
(202) 338-2026

Pasta Presto
2 Westport Square
Kansas City, Missouri 64111
(816) 756-2000

Le Petit Chef
5932 Excelsior Boulevard
Minneapolis, Minnesota 55416
(612) 926-9331

Piret's
4901 Morena Boulevard
San Diego, California 92117
(714) 274-7131

Poole's Fish Market
Chilmark, Massachusetts 02535
(617) 645-2282

Poulet
1685 Shattuck Avenue
Berkeley, California 94709
(415) 845-5932

Prime Concern
17 Middle Neck Road
Great Neck, New York 11021
(516) 487-1450

Proof of the Pudding
980 Piedmont Avenue
Atlanta, Georgia 30309
(404) 892-2359

The Providence Cheese—Tavola
Calda
407 Atwells Avenue
Providence, Rhode Island
02903
(401) 421-5653

The Public Cookshop
1630 Pine Street
Philadelphia, Pennsylvania
19103
(215) 735-7141

Rebecca's
21 Charles Street
Boston, Massachusetts 02114
(617) 742-9747

Rex's Market Delicatessen
1930 Pike Place
Seattle, Washington 98101
(206) 624-5738

Si Bon
2244 Periwinkle Way
Sanibel, Florida 33957
(813) 472-3888

The Silver Palate
274 Columbus Avenue
New York, New York 10023
(212) 799-6340

Sutton Place Gourmet
3201 New Mexico Avenue
 N.W.
Washington, D.C. 20016
(202) 363-5800

Suzanne's
1735 Connecticut Avenue
 N.W.
Washington, D.C. 20009
(202) 483-4633

*Les Trois Petits Cochons
 Charcuterie*
17 East 13th Street
New York, New York 10003
(212) 255-3844

Vivande
2125 Fillmore Street
San Francisco, California 94115
(415) 346-4430

Washington Market
162 Duane Street
New York, New York 10013
(212) 233-0250

The Watergate Chefs
2554 Virginia Avenue N.W.
Washington, D.C. 20037
(202) 298-4444

Zabar's
2245 Broadway
New York, New York 10024
(212) 787-2000

Index